LESS CERTAIN NOW

A Lifetime of Learning & Unlearning

LES AVERY

with Jennifer Clark

Less Certain Now: A Lifetime of Learning and Unlearning
by Les Avery

Printed in the United States of America

ISBN: 978-0-692-72103-2

Produced and packaged by The Michael Thomas Group
TheMichaelThomasGroup.com

Endorsements

—⚊⚋⚊—

There are those who write for profit, for a constituency, or for ego gratification and attention. Les does none of these in this remarkably candid piece. Here is a raw confrontation of a man of faith and action facing two seasons of life when things go unbearably wrong. Les' faith and spirit survive, but not without loss. Gone is the dogmatic, defensive, authoritarian, angry belief system of his youth and middle age. In its place grows the heart of an encouraging, malleable, other-centered servant. Here is seasoned spirituality, the residue of 80 years of service, study, and work that seems to cut away the myth that we can believe and accept the things of God without mental reservation.

Les proposes that God reveals himself most poignantly and productively through our own stories — that is, if we dare to be honest. He paints, from his palette of life experience, a disarming picture of an almost-finished faith — unfinished because Les' rate of insight appears to sharpen exponentially with every day he conquers after his 80th birthday. This book is experience, some of it plain, some of it mundane, some of it shocking, coming from the life of a widely acclaimed

saintly individual. The simple stories are easy to identify with. The shocking ones drive Les to take one step
beyond sight and trust vigorously the uncertainty of
the Lordship of Christ. Les matches the candor of King
Solomon as it is found in the book of Ecclesiastes. An
absorbing read indeed.

— Dave MacDonald, MA, MDiv

Most of us are fascinated to read books and watch
movies about teens and young adults "coming of age."
Les' book, *Less Certain Now* is about approaching maturity, even if we are in our 80s. I could identify with
almost every page. I suspect other readers will too. His
courage, honesty, and transparency give us all a window
into our souls and experientially demonstrate how we
truly grow relationally and develop spiritually, Enjoy!"

— Jerry Donaldson
Counselor, Former Denver Seminary adjunct faculty,
consultant and coauthor of *A House Divided*

Les Avery shines a light on the fundamentalist/
evangelical church of his upbringing, and that light
reveals a dangerous idol in the camp: the wrong kind of
certainty. Pastor Avery never rejects Jesus Christ, whom
he came to know and love in that world, but he reminds
us that our faith is just that, a faith, and that when we
turn it into the wrong kind of certainty, we tend to judge
one another, exclude one another, and then attack one
another. I thank God for Les Avery's honest story and
for his willingness to follow Christ rather than spend his
life defending a certain interpretation of the Bible and
a certain theological or denominational camp. Highly
recommended!

— Joseph Beach
Pastor of Amazing Grace Church, Denver, CO

The story of Les' life has always been an open book. He is approachable to anyone in need. It feels congruent for him to want to write down some of those stories! Les is inevitably sketching out the evolving story of his faith. With honesty and intimacy, he tells of events and relationships that have helped him to keep becoming. He is keeping the conversation going.

In this story telling, Les challenges all of his listeners to enter into the sacred place where we tell our stories. He gives us permission to blatantly put words to how we are experiencing this life that has been given us. The upshot of these conversations is a deeply theological observation: God is a God who reveals his character in hundreds/thousands of stories. The deeper the buy-in, the deeper the realization that God wants to tell us stories. And deeper yet, God wants to hear our stories about how we're doing. God is a listening God. It's how we battle against the loneliness of this hurting world. Thanks, Les, for taking us on this journey!

— John Hicks
Pastor of St. James Urban Church, Denver CO
Founder and Director of Network Coffee House,
a place for the inner-city poor to gather

—⟋⟋⟋—

*Dedicated to Thomas Avery's daughters
Ashleigh Millison and Jennifer Peppler*

Love survives all.

*And many thanks to Jennifer Clark who assisted me
in writing this book.*

Table of Contents

—⚡—

Prologue

—⁓—

The older I get the less time I have for certainty. As a young man I had more answers; I was more certain about what was true and what was false; I was more in control, more sure of myself, and had an overpowering need to be right. At 27, on the day of my ordination, my doctrinal statement took four hours to read. Maybe it was just two, but it felt like four. I sought to leave nothing out, to proclaim with certainty what I believed. Only one minister raised a question.

"If you ever depart from what you have shared with us today, will you renounce your ordination?"

I suspect I assured him I would do just that, after all I wanted to be ordained. What really was asked of me that day was to stop thinking, to never doubt. Really, at 27 years of age, did my examiners believe I arrived at absolute truth, nothing more to be learned, all wrapped up, packaged, sealed, and delivered?

Now at 85, truth seems less certain.

Some years ago William Sloane Coffin, a chaplain at Yale University from 1958 to 1975, wrote the following:

All of us tend to hold certainty dearer than the truth. We want to learn only what we already know; we want to become only what we already are. . . . Many of us have a strong allergic reaction to change — of any kind.... The result is an intolerance for nonconforming ideas that runs like a dark streak thorough human history. In religious history this intolerance becomes particularly vicious when believers divide the world into the godly and the ungodly; for then hating the ungodly is not a moral lapse but rather an obligation, part of the job description of being a true believer.

Why all this intolerance? Because while the unknown is the mind's greatest need, uncertainty is one of the heart's greatest fears. So fearful, in fact, is uncertainty that many insecure people engage in what psychiatrists call 'premature closure.' These are those who prefer certainty to truth, those in the church who put the purity of dogma ahead of the integrity of love. And what a distortion of the gospel it is to have limited sympathies and unlimited certainties, when the very reverse, to have limited certainties but unlimited sympathies, is not only more tolerant but far more Christian. The opposite of love is not hatred but fear. 'Perfect love casts out fear.' Nothing scares me like a scared people for while love seeks the truth, fear seeks safety, the safety so frequently found in dogmatic certainty, in pitiless intolerance.

There was a time when I held certainty dearer than truth, a time I claimed to be a biblical literalist, but that time has passed. I am now aware we all are selective literalists.

Knowing that, I now am less certain about truth and often spell truth in the lowercase rather than in the uppercase TRUTH.

Now I understand that just because I believe something doesn't make it true. After all, there was a time when 99.9 percent of the people in the world believed the Earth was flat. Such relief has come with understanding that just because I believe something doesn't make it true—relief at not always having to be right. Today, I am more comfortable than ever before with ambiguity, mystery, and doubt. I am comfortably living with the questions. I conclude that learning isn't the result of listening or teaching; learning is the consequence of thinking.

As I now see it, lowercase truth deals with interpretations, which includes theology, human understanding, personal beliefs. Uppercase TRUTH explains that which is scientifically verifiable but also experiential. Love should be experienced to be understood. Without experiencing love, you won't know what it means to fall in love. So uppercase TRUTH also relates one's experience of love, justice, and integrity, and what is experienced cannot be reduced to a mathematical formula. TRUTH that makes us fully human should be experienced in such powerful ways that any attempt to describe through words the experience is almost always destined to fall short.

Through stories, in the pages that follow, I seek to share part of my journey, from innocence and certainty to acceptance of what is. I seek to address the changes I've experienced throughout the years. There's little resemblance to the world of the 1930s and 40s to the world of 2016. In my reflections, I'm seeking to take you back into that world, specifically small-town America.

15

My reflections come out of my life experience, from a sheltered childhood to adulthood. They come from my experience with my gay son, Thomas, and my unorthodox wife, Jackie, both of whom did not fit the Christian mold as I was taught and both who died this past year (2015). Thomas sought and never found long-lasting contentment. He talked about grace, but struggled mightily to experience grace in his own life. Jackie did not talk about grace, but graced my life by the way she lived hers, challenged my understanding of what it meant to be a true believer and who for the most part was content with uncertainty. In this book, their stories are interwoven with mine.

A writer, I am told, should ask the question, who is your audience? Who do you picture reading that which you write? That question for years has stumped me. Recently the *aha moment* came; the light bulb went on, and I knew the answer. My audience is myself. I write to put into words my thoughts, as mixed up as they may be. I'm a guy who reflects on life-my life-and then at times puts my reflections on paper. I make no claim that my reflections are anything more than just that, reflections.

As a minister I discovered that as I shared my life through sermons and in personal conversations, people identified particularly when I shared my struggles, my pain, my doubts, my failures. Sure my life has been filled with much joy and success (as success is generally measured), but my struggles and uncertainties are what most folks identify with.

And so I conclude we connect as we share. At the level of our humanness there is union, and in that union we know we are not alone. In the connection we experience grace, and for a time the banishment of loneliness, the courage to carry on, the in-the-flesh joy of what it means to love one another.

So I ramble and tell stories and I hope maybe you can identify. Perhaps through my stories and ramblings we will connect.

Part I

The World I Came From: Small-Town America, Wellington, Ohio, in the 1930s and 1940s

Chapter 1

The Joy of Innocence

I am grateful my parents gave me a childhood. As I see it, few kids experience a childhood today. There is a push to grow up, to move on—to what I am not sure. Adulthood with all its accompanying problems comes soon enough. I suspect in this changing world, with pitfalls that did not exist in the 30s and 40s, innocence must be left behind early in life. I want to believe somehow, that is not so. For me, innocence extended well into my college years. My parents sent me to a Bible college. To be sure, the drinking as well as recreational sex that went on in secular schools also went on in Bible colleges but was not as prevalent. When I went to college there were no such things as co-ed dorms. After all, there were dorm mothers who looked out after their charges. When picking up your date at the girl's dorm you waited in the parlor under the watchful eyes of the dorm mother.

The protocol of dating was intuitively understood. You called to ask for a Friday night date on Tuesday evening, not Monday, which was too early; after all you did not want the girl to think you were too eager. You did not want to call on Wednesday because the girl might think she was an afterthought. Tuesday was just right. You waited anxiously on the phone while the girl you wanted was summoned. No phones were installed in the girl's rooms. The downstairs parlor housed the only phone for those who lived there. Finally, the voice desired was heard and the answer given. Upon hanging up, everyone in the dorm would soon know about the call.

The protocol continued for those living by the rules such as hand-holding on the first date and maybe by the third date a good night kiss, but certainly nothing much beyond that until engagement.

Not that everyone lived by such unspoken rules. A classmate once asked me about a girl I dated. He stopped me in the hall and said he was considering dating her.

"How far can I go with her?" he asked.

I was confused by the question, thinking that a full tank of gas would get him halfway to Chicago. Now that is naive innocence!

In college I sold Fuller Brushes door to door. My Fuller Brush route took me through an old, established but rundown neighborhood in Minneapolis called "Groveland." Many of the large homes were converted into apartments that rented reasonably. One fall evening found me trudging up the walk toward a brightly lit stone mansion with a red light next to the door. Lugging my Fuller Brush case, I climbed the steps and saw a woman as I glanced through the window. I could see her from the shoulders up and observed that she was reading a newspaper.

An opaque oval glass was centered in the front door. Pushing the bell I waited, but no one came to the door. Again I pushed the bell but no one appeared. Glancing back through the window, I saw the lady continuing to read the newspaper. I rang the bell again and then heard a voice calling out.

"Come in," a female voice called.

I opened the door and walked into a spacious hall as a well-dressed lady approached me. Glancing in the room to the left I froze as my heart did triple time. I could not believe my eyes. The woman I saw from the porch sat stark naked continuing to read a newspaper, totally unconcerned with my presence.

I knew immediately what I innocently walked into.

"Can I help you?" the madam asked. With my heart pounding and eyes popping, I dropped to my knees opened my Fuller Brush case and pulled out a pastry and vegetable brush. Stammering, I launched into my sales pitch.

"I have a free ga-ga-gift for you. Would you like a pa-pa-pastry brush or a ve-ve-vegetable brush?" I said. The madam looked down at me shaking her head as if she now could not believe her eyes.

"Sonny," she said, drawing out the word, "we have no use for any of your brushes around here."

Quickly closing my case, I stood and made a beeline for the door.

No doubt the place rocked with laughter as the story was told and retold of the Fuller Brush salesman country bumpkin, looking about 14 years of age who stumbled onto a house of ill repute, blushing red and falling over his words, dropped to his knees offering the madam a pastry brush or a vegetable brush. If they had known he was from the Bible school a mile away more hilarity would have shook the place.

Innocence found me lost and confused on more than one occasion, but none exceeds my sense of wide-eyed wonder and embarrassment on my one and only visit to a whorehouse.

Today teenage rebellions are daily fare. I do not remember having a decent, let alone an indecent, teenage rebellion. Some would argue that was a bad thing. Maybe I did miss out on something, after all, it took me a long time to grow up as the following three stories illustrate. Still I would not trade my growing up years in small town America in the 1930s and 40s. Innocence for all its discomfort has its place.

Bob the Robber

Of course when Bob the Robber came to live with us we didn't know he was a robber. The year was 1939, and I was all of eight years old when Bob the Robber moved in. We lived in the small town of Wellington, Ohio. Bob took over Mom's and Dad's bedroom on the first floor. Mom and Dad moved upstairs into my sister's bedroom, and we three children shared the only other upstairs bedroom. At the tail end of the Great Depression, my parents were just trying to make a little extra money to put beans on the table which is why they rented out their bedroom to Bob the Robber.

Bob the Robber was a nice guy. He was friendly, easy to be with, and he fit in well with our family. I liked Bob the Robber because he liked kids. He would hide pennies in his hair and then invite we children to dig around in his hair to find the pennies. It turned out that the pennies weren't the only things he was hiding.

Not long after he moved in, a series of robberies took place in Wellington. Boxes containing cartons of cigarettes turned up missing from some of the town's stores. The happening puzzled folks. Then one day my mother went into Bob the Robber's room, and opened the closet door. To her amazement, stacked from floor to ceiling were cartons of cigarettes!

Mom went to town to talk with Police Chief Eglin. At that time we had no telephone. Not many folks in Wellington did.

"I have a thief living in my house," she reported.

"How do you know that?" he asked.

Mom responded, "The cigarettes that are missing in town, I found in his room!"

And so a plan was set in motion to bring Bob in. Chief Eglin came to the house when Bob the Robber was at work, and he and mom set the trap.

The following Saturday, which was Bob the Robber's day off from work, mom asked Bob the Robber if he would run an errand for her. She asked him to go to the big town of Elyria, located eighteen miles from Wellington, to secure something for her. I don't remember what Mother cooked up as an excuse to get Bob the Robber out of the house for a few hours, but he was more than willing to make the Elyria trip. When everything was going according to the plan he threw her a curve.

"May I take Lester along?" Bob asked.

And I, not knowing then that Bob the Robber was a robber, begged her to let me go. I wanted more than anything else to take that ride to Elyria with him. Going to Elyria was getting to go to the big city, after all Elyria had an inconceivable number of people living there, so my dad told me, at least eighteen thousand and my dad ought to know for he worked there. Not really wanting to send her son off with a robber, but not wanting to blow the plan that she and Chief Eglin hatched, she agreed to my going along.

I sat there excitedly next to Bob the Robber as we left town. When we arrived in Elyria and picked up the item mom requested, I talked him into going over to Cascade Park so we could visit the old bear that was chained and kept in a big iron cage there. All day long he would pace back and forth, and I liked to go see him. He fascinated me.

Meanwhile back home, events took place that I would only discover in hindsight. No sooner had Bob the Robber and I left town then my mother sent my brother Kenny to town to get Chief Eglin. Kenny took the shortcut to town, running down the path next to the railroad tracks. Our house was right next to the rail-road tracks and as kids we weren't allowed to take the shortcut to town along the tracks. That route was seen as too dangerous, but this was an exception. Soon Chief Eglin and Kenny were back at the house. Then Chief Eglin confiscated the loot and set up the stake out.

My mother was deeply concerned about me, because as Chief Eglin noted, we should have returned by this time. What they didn't know was that I talked Bob the Robber into taking me to Cascade Park. Mother started to worry, certain that Bob the Robber had gotten wind of the sting and left town with me as a hostage.

She was never going to be able to forgive herself for letting me go.

"Try to be calm. We'll keep watching for them," Chief Eglin tried to reassure.

Oblivious to all of this, I was simply enjoying my Saturday at Cascade Park watching the old, chained-up bear. Bob also seemed to enjoy the bear. We were having a good time.

"We've got to go home though I know you want to stay," Bob said.

We piled in the car and unsuspectingly headed to Wellington. Everything seemed fine as we turned on Magyar Street and into the driveway, but then when the car stopped and just as Bob the Robber got out, Chief Eglin, stepped out and handcuffed Bob the Robber.

"Oh my baby!" Mom cried. My mother ran over to me and gave me a big hug, wanting to make sure I wasn't hurt. I just stood there confused by all that was happening. Chief Eglin hauled Bob the Robber off to the jail, and the arrest was the talk of the town. I felt really special to think I spent several hours with a robber just before he was arrested.

This event was the biggest thing that happened to me as a child. I never saw Bob the Robber after that, and Mother never again rented out a bedroom in our house. With a few friends, I went up to the jail to see if we might catch a glimpse of Bob the Robber through one of the windows, but we didn't see him. I felt like a pretty special kid having been with a real honest-to-goodness robber. My friends thought I was special too; they wished they knew a genuine robber, but those bragging rights were mine to cherish.

"I knew a real robber: the cigarette robber!" I bragged. "He lived with us!"

As far as I was concerned, my time spent with Bob the Robber was as great as if John Dillinger himself came to town. For a small town boy, this was as good as it gets.

First Kiss

One May evening in 1946, when I was 14 years old, my mom and dad took me to the bus depot. I boarded a Greyhound bus to travel to Montrose Bible Conference, where I was to spend the summer on the work crew. As I sat behind the bus driver, I did not sleep a wink with the excitement of that night. I was fascinated by the dark outline of the Appalachian Mountains, the squeal of the tires as the driver navigated the curves on the two-lane road. This was my first time to travel any distance from home alone.

At Montrose, I found a collection of people who viewed life through the same grid as I did, they thought like I thought. For the first time I experienced being truly liked, the first time I sensed my peers viewed me as a neat guy. I discovered the in group I needed and wanted.

My first girlfriend, Mimi, completed my days at Montrose. One of the waitresses serving on the work crew, Mimi never saw me as her real boyfriend, he was back home, a guy named Mick whom she talked warmly about now and then. Mimi and I spent time with each other during that summer. Talking to Mimi and being with her was enough. Once in a while she let me hold her hand. As the end of summer approached, the guys I bunked with started getting on me.

"Have you kissed Mimi yet?" became the question I faced each night when I returned to the dorm.

"No, but I will," I responded emphatically and nervously. I had never kissed a girl in my life, except once when playing spin the bottle I kissed Ruthie Rogers, which was not a good experience (but then I was only 10 years old).

Now the pressure was on to kiss Mimi. Not that I didn't want to kiss Mimi. I just didn't know how to go about doing so. With my masculinity at stake and the summer drawing to an end, kissing Mimi became an obsession. Only two nights remained before Mimi and I would part. In a cold sweat, uptight and tense, I found myself saying good night to her standing next to the clothesline outside the girls' dorm.

As there was no television in my childhood home — or anyone's house at that time and we did not go to the movies, my only idea of how to kiss came from pictures in magazines. I knew you closed your eyes and turned your head. Next to the clothesline, outside the girl's dorm, on the next to last night at Montrose I took aim, shut my eyes, turned my head and slammed my teeth into the top of Mimi's head. She ducked at the crucial moment.

It was embarrassing. Mimi ran into the girls' dorm. I made my way to my dorm, feeling like a failure and certain I loosened two front teeth.

The next morning after breakfast, Mimi asked if I would like to take a walk the next morning. Excitedly I agreed. Following breakfast we all would be going our separate ways. This was the last chance. So Mimi and I walked hand-in-hand down a country lane behind the conference grounds. We climbed a hill of fresh-mown hay, and on top of the hill, with the sun coming over the horizon Mimi kissed me. The kiss wasn't much as kisses go, just a gentle light brushing of lips, and yet it was wonderful, electrifying, and beautiful! All the way home, in the backseat of my dad's '41 Pontiac, I sat in a daze. Innocence was so beautiful in those days of my youth.

Carnival Sideshow

On a warm summer night in 1950, while I was home from college, my brother, Ken, my dad and I made our way to the fairgrounds. In the lazy summers of my youth something out of the ordinary like a carnival was bound to draw a big crowd in the small town of Wellington.

Walking down the midway, carnies encouraged carnival attenders to spend their money on the weird, the base, the outlandish and the absurd. One of the carnies blared through an upraised megaphone, "Come in and see the 'maphrodite." What he meant was come in and see the hermaphrodite, but he shortened it to 'maphrodite. I hadn't the foggiest idea what a hermaphrodite was, or a 'maphrodite for that matter.

Dad, Ken, and I stood in the midst of the clamor. I was trying to take it all in when Dad spoke. Shuffling his feet, stammering a bit, he spoke. "You want to go?"

"Go where?" I innocently asked.

"There," he said, with noted embarrassment nodding in the direction of the hawker outside the tent drumming up business for the viewing of the hermaphrodite.

Though I did not know what I might see, my curiosity was fully aroused. I glanced at Ken, hoping he wouldn't throw cold water on the idea. Ken was as agreeable as I was, both of us wondering if this invitation by our father was some kind of a rite of initiation. This was the closest Dad ever came to any talk about the birds and the bees and his extending an invitation to us to go with him inside that tent was obviously difficult.

Masking our own desires, Ken and I awkwardly mumbled. "If you want to go, we'll go with you."

There was a part of me that wanted to go and a part of me that didn't want to go, but I wasn't about to be left behind. Whatever I was to see inside that tent, one thing I felt certain of: this was going to stretch the boundaries of Avery propriety. Such musings did not deter the men who crowded towards the entrance, willing to hand over their money for a view of the hermaphrodite.

Not wanting to be seen and with my head lowered, I took my place in line and shuffled toward the entrance hidden behind my dad. He paused at the entrance and purchased our tickets from a woman who played the role of both ticket seller and ticket collector. I glanced at her, and my heart skipped a beat when her smoldering dark eyes met mine.

Inside the dreary tent stood a small, wooden stage. I sensed that all those in the tent felt uneasy. I knew I was uneasy. I certainly hoped that no one from the church would see the Avery boys and their dad in this sleazy place. I was aware of the restlessness of the crowd; this was not a time for chitchatting or small talk. My projection now full blown, I assumed that everyone wanted to remain unseen in that tent.

When the tent was full, the same lady who took our tickets suddenly appeared on the stage. I was startled to see her for her haunted look was burned in my mind. Apparently she did it all. She was not just the ticket taker but the main attraction as well. Without a word, for less than thirty seconds, she revealed that which identified her as a hermaphrodite. Then it was over. "That's it, boys," She said. And as quickly as she appeared, she disappeared.

The all-male crowd stood silent for a moment and then began to slip away, out of the tent and into the midway. As we left for a brief moment I lifted my eyes and glanced around at the men who were just beginning to disperse, hoping beyond hope I would not see anyone I recognized.

Now what stunned me more than what I just witnessed was the discovery that four staunch members from the church were making their way out of the tent. I saw them. Had they seen me or my brother or my dad? If they saw me, were they as jolted in seeing me as I was in seeing them? This was one of the first times in my life that I was keenly aware that the attraction to the sordid didn't pass by those of us who professed to be Christians. We wanted to believe that we were above such things—not tempted by the things that tempted lesser mortals, or if we did give into such temptations there certainly wouldn't be anyone else around.

Intuitively, I knew that we Averys, as well as the men from the church who were in that tent on that day, would not tell anyone we had been there and I knew we would not tell on them. I knew that I would never talk about what I saw. We entered into an unspoken pact of denial and cover-up, and on the following Sunday we put on our best suits and faces as we took our places in the pews. I never talked about the experience with my dad, and more than 50 years passed until I mentioned the event to my brother.

"Do you remember the summer day we went to the carnival in Wellington and saw the hermaphrodite?" I asked. After a little prodding—for there are things in life we just as soon forget—he remembered. Now we talked and laughed, together recalling our awkwardness, our youthful curiosity and our innocence and fear of discovery.

My experience on that summer afternoon as an 18-year-old boy was the extent of any sexual education I received from my father. Still, I do not feel critical of him. He did the best he could with the hand life dealt him, and that is the best any of us can do.

On that day, I really wanted to go into that tent but would never admit such and only found permission when dad suggested we all go. In a strange way, this male experience drew me closer to my father. On that afternoon, he gave me a glimpse of his human, earthy side; and I liked that side. Still there was a part of me that didn't want to go in; I was afraid. Perhaps, I thought, to go in was to betray Jesus, but more than that, I was fearful someone would see me. On that afternoon, in full denial, I figured if I didn't look around and see anyone then no one would look around and see me. Why else would one just stare at the ground?

Month Counters

In 1952 I fell in love. I mean head over heels in love. Her name was Betty, and there weren't enough hours in the day to spend with her. I was 20 and still as naïve as a child. As a junior in college, I dreaded the arrival of spring that meant the end of school when Betty would exit my life for the summer, maybe forever, as she was ambivalent about returning to college. The day school ended she departed for her home in Wadena, Minnesota, and I, with an ache in my heart, headed for my home in Ohio.

That summer I wrote every day, and she responded. I looked forward to getting home from my summer job to open the mail. Towards the end of July, Betty's letters came less frequently, but my nightly ritual of penning did not end. Then in August the Dear John letter arrived. Betty met a young man stationed at the Air Force base outside of Wadena, and she told me he was the guy for her. She had accepted his proposal of marriage.

My world came to an end on that August summer day. Sleep was nearly impossible. At best, sleep was fitful and filled with tortured dreams of loss, the loss of Betty. My appetite ceased as all food tasted like straw. For the first time in my life I knew full-blown depression.

Finally the summer ended, and with a heavy heart I headed back to college, knowing there would be no Betty to welcome me. That fall the days dragged, but male friends were there for support.

In March of that year I met Ann. In a whirlwind, we get engaged. A few months later, on August 15, 1952, we married. I turned 21 that July. That was a stormy summer marked by my first sexual experience with Ann just a couple of weeks before the wedding. At the time of the wedding, she missed her period, and we were on pins and needles fearing that she might be pregnant. Back from a brief honeymoon in northern Minnesota, our worst fear was confirmed. We were indeed expecting a baby.

Conceiving a child out of wedlock was anathema in my religious circles. The college I attended was a small fundamentalist school, and there was little doubt in my mind that if was discovered that our baby was conceived before marriage I would be asked to leave school. There was only one thing to do, and that was transfer to the University of Minnesota where I could get lost in the throng of thousands of students.

Accepted for admission at the University, I went to the school to sign up for the courses I should take in my senior year, only to be informed that not one of my credits would transfer. The University was delighted to accept me as a freshman, but that was out of the question. There was no way I could write off my first three years of college and begin again.

So I returned to the Christian college for my senior year with a plan. I attended school in the morning and worked a night shift at Folley Manufacturing in Minneapolis. I kept a low profile at school and certainly kept Ann away from school contacts so no one knew we are expecting a child. We prayed that somehow our baby would come late—just two weeks late was all that was needed. That was not too much to ask of God.

At that time, in fundamentalist evangelical circles in this country, there were month counters. If a child came prior to nine months from the time of marriage, unless that child was obviously premature, one was caught red-handed. All that was needed was nine months. John was born on March 9, a 7-pound, perfectly normal baby, not two weeks late but two weeks early; and now we were caught with our hands in the cookie jar. Somehow the powers that be at the school were unaware of the birth, and in early May I graduated, having avoided the dishonor of what I believed would be expulsion.

With our baby boy, we headed for Ohio for the summer, unsure of what we were going to do with our lives. Furthermore, we were headed right into the center of a family of fundamentalists who were not about to be fooled by my simply saying, "I don't understand it, but the baby just arrived early." After all, most of them, my aunts and uncles who lived in the area, were at our wedding. They knew no 7-pound baby arrives early; the child obviously was conceived before our marriage.

One family member in particular was on to us. My Aunt Ruth, who served as a missionary in South America, was home on furlough, and she was not buying the lie that the baby just came early. Aunt Ruth and Aunt Esther, a nurse, were not fooled for a minute and were rather insistent that a terrible sin had been committed. They wanted me to go forward at the Baptist church and confess my sin, believing that unless I did that God would never bless me. My mother was just confused, or *torn* is a better word. She in her heart knew that intercourse happened before marriage but sought to explain to her sisters that I never lied to her before, so I must not be lying now.

In July I learned of Denver Seminary, a new school then known as Conservative Baptist Seminary. That July, I was accepted via a phone interview, so Ann and I, with our baby boy, headed for Denver in August. Coming to Denver promised to be a new lease on life. No one knew us. We could make new friends, and no one would inquire about when we were married. On the rare occasion one did, we simply lied and moved our wedding to July 15 instead of August 15. After all, no one ever asked to see a wedding license.

I loved seminary. I loved the classes and the guys (the student population was all males studying to be ministers). Yet this dark secret about the birth of our son nagged at me. The awareness that I was living a life of deception ate away at me. Courting a nervous breakdown, I went to the dean of the seminary, Dr. Vernon Grounds, to tell him I was dropping out of school. He sat me down and gently probed. In tears I poured my heart out to him.

"I am not fit to be a minister," I said. "I have committed this terrible sin. I had sex before marriage and I have lied, and I am dropping out of school." To my surprise, he took me in his arms and held me until my crying stopped.

"I want you to hear two things," he said. "First, as an agent of Jesus Christ I want you to know you are forgiven, and secondly, I do not want you to drop out of school."

Dr. Grounds' desire for me to stay in seminary overwhelmed me more than the truth that I was forgiven. Is there really forgiveness without reconciliation, restoration? This I do know. That time with Dr. Grounds was the very first time I was consciously aware of God's overwhelming love for me. I was well schooled in the wrath of God, but that day in Dr. Grounds' office was a never-to-be-forgotten experience of God's love pouring over my life.

Chapter 2

The Danger of Innocence

The Deadly Games We Played

I found myself doing a double take as I viewed the headline of an article on the *Denver Post* front page a few years ago informing the readership that the playground game of Tag had been outlawed in a Colorado Spring elementary school. Tag outlawed? *This must be some kind of a joke*, I thought. But this wasn't April's Fool's Day, and sure enough, it wasn't a spoof or a misprint. No longer were kids permitted to play Tag on the school grounds of this elementary school.

A little research revealed that the Colorado Springs school was not the only school in America where Tag was outlawed. I discovered Tag was forbidden in elementary schools in Cheyenne, Wyoming, Spokane Washington, Charleston, South Carolina, and Attleboro, Massachusetts.

How did any of us old-timers manage to grow up without being permanently maimed? I can see banning the old school yard game Crack the Whip. If you were at the end of that line, your feet would go out from under you and you went sailing head over heels when the whip made of kids raced around the schoolyard. Maybe the game Red Rover should be banned if any kids play that in schoolyards these days. I can still feel the sting of some kid bigger than me slamming into my wrists as they were entwined vice griping the neighboring wrist. But Tag, that seemed harmless enough

Of course someone could fall and break an arm or otherwise get injured. Such a risk is taken by any of us whenever we step outdoors. No, not when we step out outdoors, but when we get out of bed. After all the greatest number of accidents I understand are house-hold accidents.

What about all the other games we played as kids, games now relegated to the dustbins of history with the advent of television, computers and cell phones? How about Hide and Seek, or Ollie, Ollie Oxen Free, where you threw the ball over the roof of the barn and raced around to the other side to tag the person trying to retrieve it? How many times did I come close to a head-on collision when running full force while the person who caught the ball was running in the opposite direction around the same corner of the barn seeking to get to home base?

How did any of us manage to grow up? After all, we rode bikes without helmets, played pickup football games without pads, ran around barefoot from June through August, played basketball in haylofts of barns lighted by an extension cord with a screwed-in 75-watt light bulb, roamed freely the streets of our home towns from age six on, built rafts and set sail on them in any muddy swamp we could find, swam in streams and ponds and lakes found surrounding the town. What kept us from concussions, fires, electrocuting ourselves, or drowning?

In the book *God, But I'm Bored!*, Eileen Guder writes:

"You can live on bland food so as to avoid an ulcer, drink no tea or coffee or other stimulants in the name of health, go to bed early and stay away from night life, avoid all controversial subjects so as to never give offense, mind your own business and avoid involvement in other people's problems, spend money only on necessities and save all you can. You can still break your neck in the bathtub, and it will serve your right."

Certainly wisdom mandates and I am all for helmets for cyclists and pads for those who participate in sports or pick-up games. I am for safe lighting minimizing the danger of fire in haylofts housing basketball hoops. I suspect few haylofts sport basketball hoops in 2016, and who swims in streams or ponds these days?

Back to the outlawing of Tag. I believe kids today are missing out on the joy of imagination and exploration as they spend most of their time sitting on their behinds playing computer games or watching television. Sure we took some foolish risks; kids do that.

For all of that I would not exchange my childhood for that of my grandchildren. I'd say growing up in small-town America was wonderful. As a kid, all of nature beckoned, and I never remember saying to my parents, "I'm bored." There was always that wonderful world in and around my hometown to explore.

When Experts Blow It

As a kid growing up in the 30s and 40s, I didn't question authority figures. Kids wouldn't think of addressing grown-ups by their first name. Kids were to be seen and not heard, at least not heard in any serious way. At family gatherings, kids often ate separate from adults. An order from an adult was to be obeyed, not challenged. At the top of the list of never-to-be-questioned adults were doctors, lawyers, teachers, ministers. Perceived as experts their word was law.

Now, on the backside of life, I've learned experts aren't always that expert. I listen to authorities and ask what qualifies this person as an expert? I often wonder if it isn't just chutzpah. Years ago someone defined an expert as follows: "X is the unknown quantity and spurt is a drip under pressure." To my old ears such a definition now sounds sophomoric, but there may be some truth in it.

It is nice to be regarded as an expert, to be looked up to and seen as one whose views are wise. I am amused at how wise I am considered since I passed the magic age of 70. Some people even use the description wise when describing me. I don't recall anyone applying that word to me in my 50s and 60s. I am amused because I am saying, for the most part, the same things I always said.

In my lifetime, experts were often wrong. When my parents took me to a nationally renowned doctor, an expert on back problems, he told my parents they had a lazy boy who refused to straighten up. That expert got it wrong. I had Scheuermann's disease; in my case a disease that wasn't diagnosed until I was in my 40s. Scheuermann's is a form of kyphosis, which attacks boys between the ages of 12 and 14. Later, another medical expert told me I probably would be in a wheelchair by the time I reached 30. I'm glad he was wrong.

When one of my sons was in first grade, an expert, a social worker recently out of graduate school told me he was a slow learner and should be held back. Believing she was an expert, he was held back. The following year her counsel was the same. From her viewpoint, a third trip through first grade was in order. This social worker didn't have children of her own, and yet because she held a degree in social work I believed she knew best, so my boy again repeated first grade. Then low and behold a discovery! The kid wasn't slow at all. He was dyslexic. The by-product of her advice made schooling for him extremely painful. At 19, still in high school, two years behind others his age, life was difficult.

In seminary, an expert told me that a preacher should never talk about himself from the pulpit. "People don't come to hear your story. They come to hear God's story," he said. Years later, I discovered that when I shared my life, my joys and hurts, people identified. They loved when I let them in on my struggles, because they could identify. I found out, contrary to the expert's wisdom, that my story is God's story. God has always told his story through people like you and me. The Bible is full of stories about how ordinary people experienced, or didn't experience, God.

Maybe the only unique thing I have to share with folks is my story, wherein I experienced success and failure, a sense of God's presence and absence. Interesting that many of my teachers and most professors in seminaries across the land possess little or no experience shepherding a congregation. It is not uncommon to hear professors in other disciplines with little or no hands-on experience telling others how to do it.

There is one place where the title "expert" fits me. I am an expert on Les Avery. I lived every minute of his life. I don't know everything there is to know about him, but I know more about him than anyone else. Knowing what I have learned about experts, I wonder why I allowed others to tell me how to live my life, what I ought to do, and where I ought to go, what I ought to say, how I ought to think, and what I need to believe. These days I am leery of anyone who says, "I know this is best for you." Such a statement presumes the expert has foresight and knows exactly how life will all come out. I believe such wisdom belongs only to God.

Several years ago I attended a writer's conference. I desired to be a better writer. I wanted to learn more about crafting words. A voice inside said, "Les, you have been about the business of writing for 65 years. You've authored several thousand sermons." I tend to dismiss that voice. Still, could it be that I know more about writing than I want to own? While staying open to learning, I intend to not let the criticism of experts determine my worth as a writer. You as the reader will determine that.

Although it may not sound like it, I welcome experts in every arena of life, but I want them to partner with me for joint problem-solving. My confession is that I am often too willing to unquestioningly enter into blind obedience. I suspect I am not alone.

Subtle Superiority

Peter was three days old when he came to live with us. His momma, my Aunt Treva, died giving birth to him. Caught in an Ohio blizzard, Uncle Irvin got her to the hospital too late. My Aunt Treva hemorrhaged and died. The fact that Peter was a big baby, weighing 12 pounds, only compounded the risk. To top it off, Aunt Treva had not gone to a doctor during her pregnancy. The family was dirt poor. Uncle Irvin and Aunt Treva still owed the doctor for their last child, so Aunt Treva was too embarrassed to go. The year was 1945, and Peter was her sixth child.

Before Aunt Treva died, we played with our cousins every Tuesday in the summertime. That was when Aunt Treva came to do the washing. They didn't own a washing machine, and so she used ours. We didn't see much of our cousins after my aunt died, though they lived only five miles out of town. You see, Uncle Irvin was a drunk. When we stopped by after Aunt Treva died, we never knew whether he would be drunk or sober, and so after a few visits, we stopped going.

Jane, the oldest child, tried desperately to hold the family together, but then she was only 16, two years older than I was, and still in high school. Yet, in spite of Jane's attempts to hold the family together after Aunt Treva's death, this was not to be. Ultimately, the family split up, and the children were farmed out to friends and family members. We adopted Peter, and thus he took on the Avery name. He became my brother.

I lost track of my cousins as the months rolled into years. During those years of no contact I heard that Jane's son, Jack, committed suicide. I got Jane's address and wrote her offering my condolences, but she never responded to my letter. In 1983, I accepted an invitation to preach at the little country church my parents attended in Penfield, Ohio. To my delight, my cousin Jane showed up. She came to hear her cousin preach though she hadn't darkened the door of a church since the death of her mother. After the service I invited her to join our family for dinner. She came to the very same house where we played together when we were kids while her mom did the washing.

The house where I grew up was small, and there were a lot of people visiting that day. There was no place to sit, all the chairs were taken; so Jane and I found a corner in the kitchen and sat on the floor and talked. She spoke of her son's suicide, her daughter's cancer, her recent divorce, of her determination to keep the family together and her sadness of being unable to do so.

Finally, she got to the silent years, all those years when we had no contact. "You stopped coming to see us because my dad was an alcoholic," she said. The words were like an arrow piercing my heart. Speechless, I nodded for she was right on target. Truth was spoken and truth hurt. "You took Peter, but you could have had all of us," she said. "We knew it was not possible to come and live with you, but we needed loving, too."

"There were nights when my dad went out to drink . . . I would push the dresser in front of my bedroom door because I knew he would try to come into my room to fondle me when he stumbled home. But with the resistance of the dresser he would wander down the hall to his bedroom." Then came the punch line never to be forgotten. "For all of that," she said, "my father taught me what your father never taught you." She paused and then added, "He taught me not to be prejudiced."

I offered no rebuttal. Prejudice did mark our lives growing up. We felt *better than — better than* blacks, Jews, unbelievers, anyone else who did not agree with our fundamentalist religion. We believed we were *better than* those unwashed in the water of cleanliness and in the blood of the Lamb. Exclusion, not inclusion, separated us from all who did not agree with us.

Overwhelmed, I sat at a loss for words. Then Jane reached out and took my hands in hers and broke the silence. "Something good came out of it," she said. Now I found my voice.

"What possible good could come out of the drunkenness of your father, the death of your son, your daughter's cancer, your divorce and our abandoning you after your mom died?"

She responded with just three words. "I found you," and once again I was speechless. She found me, and I didn't know she was even looking. Of course she wasn't talking about literally finding me. Truth be told, we found each other. The words I like to use are "soul mates." Jane is one of those few individuals one finds in a lifetime where connection becomes union, where realness and honesty prevails and there is no need for small talk. That is what happened on that Sunday afternoon as we sat knee to knee in a corner of the kitchen. We truly found each other

Cream Rises to the Top

I was born five minutes ahead of my twin sister, Esther. She was smarter, better looking, and quicker than me. I know this because while growing up in school together we were compared to our faces.

At home, we were told we were only average. Mom advised us not to think too highly of ourselves. "Pride cometh before a fall, so do not think too highly of yourself. Remember you are only average." So I lived that out, and through high school earned mostly *C*'s. That's average; Mom would be pleased, I thought.

Yet, for all of that, there remained the contradictory message that because we knew Jesus, accepted him as our personal savior, we were *better than* some other folks in town. After all, we didn't dance, smoke, drink, play cards or go to movies. We were set apart, *better than* others — certainly better than the worldly folks all around us, the unsaved. Obviously to my mind at that time, to be saved was to be *better than*, right?

So as I wrestled with inadequacy and the confusing message that I was only average, while at the same time knowing that I was *better than*, I became quick to reject praise and skeptical when it was given. Particularly in seminary, I yearned to have all the answers while keenly aware that I was only average.

I nearly failed Greek, which was essential to graduating; but study as I did — hour after hour, the struggle felt futile. I spoke up in class, asked questions, made comments; but the barely-passing grades continued. Now I am not average and getting *D*s, and a *D* is below average, and that deeply troubled me.

Jack, my best friend in seminary was also enrolled in Greek, said, "You are raising too many questions," he said. "Sit in the front row, and keep your mouth shut. You might get a better grade." Following his suggestion I discover to my delight that my grade went from a *D* to a *B* in a short span of time. All I was aware of doing differently was not asking questions and sitting in the front row. One would think that Greek would hardly be a subjective course, but so much for objectivity!

A few years later, I returned to the seminary with other graduates for an afternoon of interaction with the seniors who were about to leave school and enter the field of ministry. I sat with 10 other graduates, all of us now local ministers, fielding questions asked by the senior students. "Now that you are writing sermons weekly, do you find yourself using Greek?" one asked. The gathered alumni began to respond, and the responses were diplomatic going along this order. "I haven't used it, but I intend to use it," or "I should use it but I find myself not using my Greek." I was the last to respond. "I don't use it. I don't intend to use it, and I do not see how Greek has any relevance for twentieth-century ministry." I proclaimed.

At the time, I thought my answer was so profound. I cut to the chase, told it like it was. Now I see my answer as shameless arrogance. Sitting in that room on that day was my old Greek professor, and he did not appreciate my response.

It was, as I recall, in a subsequent encounter with him and in the presence of several other seminarians that he said, "Les, cream rises to the top, and you are not cream." Now that smarted. Truthfully, I never regarded myself as cream using his analogy. neither did I regard myself as skim milk, though two percent sounded about right as that fit my idea of average. Needless to say, the battle cry had been sounded, and my relationship with my Greek professor was less than compatible.

For years, we didn't speak and when accidentally meeting ignored each other. Then one day to the surprise of both of us we met in a hospital room where a mutual friend of ours lay dying which was an awkward moment. After a perfunctory exchange of greeting he left, and in few minutes I also exited only to find him still waiting for an elevator to arrive. As the two of us descended on the elevator I said, "Dr. Burdick I hear such positive remarks about your teaching these days. As you near retirement I hope you know how much you are appreciated and revered."

He brightened up. "Some people said that to you?" he asked.

"Yes they believe you are a great teacher," I replied. We exited the elevator and chattered amiably for a short time before departing.

In that affirming exchange something beautiful happened. Affirmation does make a difference and in this case reconciliation took place. A few years later as he himself lay dying I visited him and all was well between us.

Chapter 3

Doing It All Right and Getting It All Wrong

"It is absolutely right to love and learn from the sixty-six books of the Bible, but it is wrong to fear their every word, for everything biblical is not Christ like. For example: 'Now go smite Amalek ...do not spare them, but kill both man and woman, infant and suckling, ox and sheep, camel and ass...Thus says the Lord' (see I l Samuel 15:3). Besides, we Christians believe in the Word made flesh not in the Word

*made words. And for Gods' sake let's be done with
the hypocrisy of claiming, 'I am a biblical literalist'
when everyone is a selective literalist, especially those
who swear by the anti-homosexual laws in the book of
Leviticus and then feast on barbecued ribs and delight
in Monday night football for it is toevah, an abomination, not only to eat pork but merely to touch the skin
of a dead pig."* — William Sloan Coffin

I'm Not a Homosexual

In the mid 60s I found myself at the Pastor Counseling
Institute in Athens, Georgia, for a 10-day intensive
lab experience. My twin sister and her husband, who
was an Army chaplain, had gone and found it such
a powerful experience they paid my way to go. The
mornings were spent listening to informative lectures
about human behavior, and the afternoons were spent
in small groups.

One afternoon, the 17 people in attendance (15 men
and two women) gathered in a meadow for an assign-
ment. We were instructed to choose a partner and
look deeply into our partner's eyes for three minutes
without looking away. We were to convey, without
speaking, a message of some kind to our partner. A
message of caring, disinterest, frivolity, whatever. The
choice was ours.

If I am going to look into anyone's eyes for three
minutes, I want it to be a woman's. And so, when the
signal was given to seek a partner, I made a beeline for
one of the two females, but before I could get to either of
them, someone else chose them. And thus by default, I
found myself with Harvey, a Presbyterian minister from
Texas, and endured the longest three minutes of my life!
Harvey was coming on to me like gangbusters! I knew

looking into his eyes what he was thinking, *Les, I love you!* It was more than I could take. I knew he was queer. I found myself looking at the sky; I could not meet his intense gaze. Finally, the dreaded experience ended, and Harvey, aware of my discomfort, said, "You want to take a walk?" I responded, uptight and defensively. "No! If the group walks I walk, but otherwise no."

Shortly after that exercise, we went back into our small groups. Harvey was not in my group, and so when asked about our experience in the meadow, I was able to talk freely about him. I told the group that Harvey was certainly coming onto me, and I didn't appreciate it for one minute. When I finished talking, the group leader looked at me and asked a question that floored me.

"Les, are you a homosexual?" I felt anger surface in me. "What? Me? A homosexual? You can't be serious! If anyone is a homosexual, Harvey is," I retorted.

"Tell me, Les," the group leader said, "Have you ever had a homosexual experience?" Taken back, I once again emphatically stated that I had no time for homo-sexuals. Gently, the leader pressed on. So I relayed an experience when I was 12 years old.

One afternoon, when I went to town, I passed the music store where an 18-year-old whom I recognized but whose name I do not remember stopped me and said, "You know I have something for you. I have a pair of pants that I know will fit you." This young man lived around the corner from us, and I was taken aback by his kindness. In my naiveté, How nice, I thought, that he wanted to give me a pair of pants. And so I went into the music store. "Here," he said. "Take these pants and go back in the bathroom and try them on; I think they will fit you perfectly." Then he added, "I'll come with you and we'll see how they look."

And so, back to the bathroom we went. No one else was around. Wellington was a quiet, lazy, little town so there were in most stores, long periods of time with no customers. I dropped my pants and prepared to step into the trousers he handed me, then he made his move. As I grew distraught, I started begging him to leave me alone, and he backed off. I quickly pulled up my pants and bolted from the bathroom. But I didn't leave the music store until he wrapped up the gift of the pants he promised to give me.

When I got home I told my parents what happened. At that time, I didn't know the meaning of the word *homosexual*. My father turned white as a ghost and stormed out of the house. Later, I learned he went to the music store, and I think might just have beaten that 18-year-old within an inch of his life, but the kid wasn't there. Instead, he confronted the owner of the store, who blew off the incident.

On that afternoon in Athens I related several other times when I was older that I was propositioned. Once, while waiting at a stoplight, I glanced at a man at the wheel of the car next to me, who, in a crude and vulgar way, was looking lustfully at me and making obscene gestures with his mouth and hands. Another time, I hitchhiked home from college on a bitterly cold November day. Just outside of South Bend, Indiana, a car stopped and the driver matter-of-factly stated he would take me as far as Toledo if I agreed to spend an hour with him in a motel room. I declined, and he drove off.

There was still another time when sharing a motel room at a clergy gathering when I was propositioned by a pastor. He was the father of five, a nice man. We shared a room to save money. When we went to bed that night he came on to me—big time. The next day, he was apologetic, and I never outed him.

I finished by assuring the group I was not a homosexual. I assured them I could not stand being around them. Then the group leader once again spoke.

"Les, a man looks in your eyes as he is told to do and conveys a message of tenderness and caring and you want to make him out to be a homosexual. *Who* has the problem?"

I felt my world reel around me. Harvey only did what he was asked to do, and I concluded he was gay. In my family of origin, public displays of tenderness and love toward other men by men were not acceptable. Men were to be tough: no tears, no softness. Suck it in and forge on; that was the unspoken message.

The following days at the Institute I wrestled with my homophobia. From time to time, the group worked with me on this issue. Toward the end of our time there, the group leader asked me yet another question.

"If you were propositioned by a woman, how would you feel?" My response was, "I think I would be flattered. It would be nice to know that someone else found me desirable.

"What's the difference?" he asked. "Can't you say to a man that may proposition you, 'Thanks, but no thanks'? Why must you call him names and put him down? If you are secure in your own sexuality, you won't be threatened by someone else's."

That time at the Pastoral Counseling Institute was a stretching, growing time for me. Little did I know that within a few short years, my son, Thomas, would come out to me. Now I see how God was preparing me, forcing me to face my hatred and homophobia.

It was the beginning of my lifelong journey of wrestling with the issue of homosexuality.

My Gay Son

As I sat at the doctor's office with my adult son, he filled out a form that called for his date of birth. September 23, 1955, he wrote. Somehow as that date entered my consciousness, I found myself fighting back tears. I thought about his birth and all the hopes and dreams wrapped up in his arrival.

On that fall day, when Ann went into labor, we rushed to Porter Hospital in south Denver and were met by our doctor. I was invited into the delivery room to be present for this birth, a new idea at the time. "Now, don't block the view of the father," The doctor instructed the attending nurses. A mirror strategically placed allowed me to watch the birth of my son while standing at the head of my wife. Not only was I in the delivery room, but I was invited to administer the anesthesia. The doctor showed me the facemask and asked me to place it over Ann's nose and mouth when the pain became acute. I was to watch her closely and when she relaxed after a few seconds I was to take the facemask away which is exactly what I did.

"It's a boy!" the doctor proudly declared, and so Thomas Peter Avery was born.

In 1955, I was 24 years old and a middler at Denver Seminary. It never dawned on me that there would be any problems with this dear, innocent, helpless, beautiful little baby boy. I just took it for granted that he would grow up to be a normal kid and live a relatively problem-free life. Good kids came from good homes, and Ann and I came from good Christian homes. My parents loved me dearly, and I found such warmth and strength in their love. I fully expected that Thomas' childhood would be just like mine.

Thomas was our second son. His older brother, John, was two when Thomas was born. After Thomas, came Ned three years later; and then in 1964, God gave us a girl, our Jennifer. In 1968, we adopted a 9-month-old girl, Jodi, who stole our hearts. We believed that everything would turn out perfectly with these dear children.

Tom's childhood just passed by. There was nothing spectacular or problematic about his young years. He was easy to ignore, being very compliant. In fact, I don't remember much about his childhood. I do remember wanting him to be rough and tumble, but he wanted to play with dolls. I signed him up to play peewee football, but he often skipped practice. Thomas rolled in the dirt before coming home so I would believe he was at practice.

At the time, I was a youth pastor at a Baptist church and loved every aspect of my job. I wanted to serve God. In fact, I placed God first, not family. (You can convince yourself that you are serving God when maybe what you're doing is actually self-centered.) Now, I suspect I loved those four years (from 1957-61) because I was growing up myself. I was actually a kid with the title of pastor playing with and enjoying other kids!

I don't remember being that concerned about Thomas. He was determined to please, easy to be around and easy to ignore. Thomas was kind and caring; there was not a mean bone in his body. By the time the girls came along, Thomas served as a natural babysitter. We often left him with the younger children. He appeared to enjoy playing the role of parent, and we willingly allowed him to do so.

I wish I could live those years over again, for there is much I would do differently.

Thomas was especially close to his mother, and right through high school the two of them enjoyed long and significant talks. They enjoyed each other's company. Thomas was far more sensitive than his older brother, John. He was frail and far more artistic. Already, not known to me, he was struggling with his attraction to boys. He knew he was different, and his difference confused him.

It was years later that I learned that Thomas' first homosexual experience occurred when he was a 12-year-old child with some neighbor boys. Thomas shared none of this with us at the time. He appeared to be interested in girls in high school and dated. We had every reason to believe he would marry some fine Christian girl and live his life out in a house on a hill with a station wagon in the driveway and smoke drifting lazily out of the chimney.

Both Ann and I were totally unprepared for the 60s. Life in the 50s was predictable, with right and wrong clearly definable. Now, in the mid 60s, our lives began to unravel. The hippie movement raged across America. Drugs became a way of life for so many teenagers. I didn't even know the meaning of the word marijuana until I discovered my oldest son, John, was not only using but was dealing. There were knocks on his basement bedroom window, and I, in my naiveté, believed other kids were the guilty ones. John also introduced his two younger brothers to drugs. In fact, he became one of the primary drug dealers at Cherry Creek High School. Almost before we were aware of what was happening, we lost control of our son.

By this time, I was serving as the founding pastor of a new church development. I loved the challenge of being wrapped up in the growth of a thriving, new Baptist church. I didn't spend a lot of time with the family. Then, I felt that they should understand that I was doing the Lord's business. So there were those occasions, too many of them, when I allowed parishioners to interrupt a family gathering. Too many times I cancelled time with my kids because of something that came up at the church. There were sermons to prepare, committee meetings to attend, boards to serve on. I was on my way up the ladder in ministry, and the family was supposed to understand that.

When Thomas came out of the closet at 18, I was stunned by his announcement. By that time, my world was rapidly coming undone. All three of my boys were on drugs, and my marriage was in serious trouble—a divorce pending. Facing this collapse of my world, I wanted out of the institutional church. I knew I could no longer be the answer man. I didn't have answers for my own life, let alone someone else's. I also knew that as a divorced minister, there would be no place for me in the denomination I was then identified with.

Feelings About the Church

I haven't always had a hate/love affair with the church. Truth be told, the church has been wonderfully good to me, and I have been blessed to serve the church for the better part of 60 years. Because I've been connected with the church for most of my life, I feel entitled to evaluate the church in a somewhat objective fashion. My quarrel with the church is not a new one but a personal one that comes after years of reflection.

I was saved when I was nine years old. Getting saved was a high priority in my family. Each year, a weeklong evangelistic service was held in the church of my youth. Essential was an evangelist from out of state. Somehow an evangelist from Indiana or Michigan offered more authenticity than a speaker from a neighboring town in Ohio. Jesus seemed to understand when he said, "A prophet has no honor in his own country." Thus the Reverend Van Gilder from far-away Michigan came to conduct the week of evangelistic services at First Baptist in the summer of 1940.

Of course the stated purpose of such meetings was to win the lost to Christ. The problem was, with few exceptions, the lost never attended the advertised meetings. The faithful were there to be sure, and in-spite of the fact that few (if any) unsaved were present, the evangelist was not deterred from delivering hellfire and brimstone messages — messages that quite literally scared the hell out of me.

I sat with my family as Reverend Van Gilder spoke of burning eternally in hell if you did not accept Christ as your personal savior. My heart was pounding as if threatening to jump out of my chest. At the end of an evangelistic sermon an altar call must be extended even if no unbelievers were present. So as the first verse of "Just As I Am" was sung, barely before the first note could be sounded, in tears and fearful that I was going to burn in hell, I raced down the aisle and was enthusiastically welcomed by the Reverend Van Gilder. I was the only one who responded to the altar call that night.

Terrified that my confession of faith the first night was inadequate as the Reverend Van Gilder's hellfire and brimstone sermons boomed forth each night — and to be absolutely sure that I was saved once and for all — I fled down the aisle at the altar call three nights running. Whereas the first night I was enthusiastically welcomed, the following two nights found my reception going from cool to cold. Sitting alone in the room next to the sanctuary crying and ignored by the evangelist, I soon became aware of my mother's arms around me, assuring me that I was indeed saved.

For years following that experience, the date I was saved in the summer of 1940 was inscribed in the flyleaf of my Bible. Somehow writing that date down in your Bible was important. Reflecting on that experience three quarters of a century later I see things differently. I now see what happened on those three nights as child abuse. To hang a nine-year-old over the flames of hell and talk about eternal burning thus frightening him so much that three nights straight he answers an altar call in tears certainly must be some form of abuse. So my coming to Jesus was out of fear, the first element in the church's control over me.

The second element of the church's control over me was guilt. Guilt was a relative stranger to me until the onset of puberty, an onset that came late and that I was totally unprepared for. I had no idea what was happening to my body. I had no warnings of new physical drives. I did not know there was even such a thing as puberty let alone what the word meant. Anything related with sex or bodily functions in our family was ignored or dealt with in a coded language. For example, *Number One* and *Number Two* dealt with bodily waste, and I knew that *in a family way* meant someone was pregnant.

No one had to tell me when I experienced my first nocturnal omission or wet dream that some awful sin occurred. Once I discovered the pleasure of masturbation, my guilt was compounded with the certainty that I committed the unpardonable sin. Masturbation and intercourse where forbidden words in my world.

Convinced as a 14-year-old that I was the only person in the universe who struggled with such sins, I was comforted several years later when a friend shared, "Ninety-nine out of a hundred boys masturbate and the other is a liar." I couldn't believe my ears! Somebody uttered the word out loud and whether what he said was true or not, I was overwhelmingly relieved to know that I was not the only one in the world wrestling with sexual drives. Being a born-again Christian, the only thing I knew about sex as a young boy was that it was wrong. Of course, that all changed with marriage, although I was not sure how something so wrong suddenly became so right. But who was I to question the powers that be?

So the church controlled my behavior first by fear and then by guilt. The third way the church of my youth controlled me was through shame, the shame I wrote about in an earlier chapter—the shame that came from having sex before marriage that resulted in the conception of my oldest son, John.

Fear, guilt, and shame resulted in absolute control by the fundamentalist, evangelical church. As I look back I am convinced that the control (resulting from fear, guilt and shame) was not intentional. The ministers and youth leaders simply lived out what they were taught. They lived it out as I lived it out—by acting and thinking "if we trust Jesus everything would be wonderful." Basically, we were pretending though we didn't think we were.

Furthermore, I believed that others did not deal with the same temptations that plagued my life. Now I am fully aware that their issues were mostly like mine, and that the ministers and youth leaders of my childhood were not living the perfect problem-free lives they presented.

This business of control through fear, guilt and shame continues in many churches today. I used to easily condemn other religions, particularly Muslims who strap explosives to their bodies and in the name of Allah blow themselves up killing countless others. I am sure they are brainwashed. Then one day I began to wonder why I did not think I had been brainwashed.

When I attended youth rallies as a young man, preachers challenged us to lay down our lives, if need be, for Christ. My answer (underscored sometimes by going forward to dedicate my life to full-time Christian service) was a clear "yes." I am chilled to realize that in my teens if someone I admired, one of the ministers who I gave control of my life to, told me that I needed to lay down my life for the cause of Jesus, I would have willingly done so, maybe even by blowing myself up.

Chapter 4

When Getting It All Wrong Turned Out All Right

Ethel Wants To Die

One Sunday morning, my friend Elaine approached me after the church service. "Pastor, would you please visit a friend of mine who is in a nursing home in Thornton? She is in her 80s, and she has stopped eating. She is growing weaker and weaker, and no one on the staff can get her to eat. Her name is Ethel, and she is telling everybody she wants to die."

I did not know Elaine's friend, so I asked, "Why do you want me to visit her?"

"I just know that if you talked to her she would start eating," Elaine responded.

"I am not a miracle worker. Don't put that on me," I protested. Elaine persisted and I resentfully agreed to make the visit.

To my shame I put off going for several days and then feeling guilty climbed into the car and headed for Thornton. The church I served was located in Littleton, a suburb on the south side of Denver, and Thornton is a suburb on the north side. By the time I located the nursing home and made my way into the lobby, 45 minutes passed since leaving the church.

The lady at the desk in the lobby directed me to Ethel's room. The door was closed, and so I knocked. An aide responded to my tapping. When I introduced myself as Elaine's pastor and told her I came to visit Ethel, her face broke into a huge smile.

"We have been waiting for you. Elaine has told us all about you and somehow I know you can get Ethel to eat," she said. All I wanted to do was turn around and run. "Let me tell Ethel you are here," she said as she closed the door, leaving it slightly ajar.

As I stood in the hallway, this is the conversation I heard coming from inside Ethel's room. "Elaine's minister has come to see you. Isn't that nice of him?"

"I don't want to see him!" Ethel snapped.

"Now Ethel," the aide continued, "he has driven all the way from Littleton. He is a very busy man. Certainly you are going to be kind enough to see him."

"I told you I don't want to see him!!" Ethel shouted even more emphatically than before. Then I heard the voice of the aide change. No longer was it sweet and demure.

"Ethel you don't have a choice in this—you are going to see him whether you want to or not!" Then I heard the footsteps of the aide as she approached the door. With the same disarming smile as before she said to me, "Come on in. I will leave you two alone. I will be at the nursing station if you should need me." She headed down the hall, turned the corner and was gone.

I walked to Ethel's bed wishing I was anywhere but in this place, with no clue of what to do or say. She was lying on her side, her face to the wall, her back to me. Then I found myself saying, "Ethel, I am told that you want to die." She did not move or speak. "Ethel, I am going to pray right now that you will die. I am going to ask Jesus to come and carry you to Heaven in his arms this very day."

Now there is movement. Ethel slowly rolled over and looking up at me she asked, "You would do that for me?"

"Yes. I'll do that. It is all right with me if you die," I said.

"I want so much to die, but they won't let me. They keep trying to force me to eat. They tell me I have to go on living in this place, but I don't want to. I am ready to die. I don't want to stay here any longer. I just want to go home and be with the Lord," Ethel said.

I reached down and took Ethel's right hand and said, "Reach up with your other hand and slip it into the hand of Jesus." With Ethel clinging to my one hand and feebly reaching toward the ceiling with the other, I prayed that she might die. When I finished, I bent over, kissed her on the forehead and quietly slipped out of the room, heading down the hall in the opposite direction of the nursing station. Finding a side exit I bolted through the door and headed for my car.

For the next few weeks I avoided Elaine. I knew I let her down. Then one Sunday, there she was directly in front of me. Feeling guilty, I asked her about Ethel, knowing she would tell me that she was dead. "Les, what did you say to that woman?" Elaine said. Before I could defensively respond, she continued, "The entire staff thinks you are some kind of a miracle worker. I knew you would make a difference. Why, no more than 15 minutes after you left, Ethel buzzed the nursing station and asked for a meal, and she has been eating ever since!"

Now I was speechless, and then in a flash I knew. In spite of myself on that afternoon when I resisted going to see her, Ethel experienced me as taking her desire to die seriously. Often the best we can offer others is the gift of presence. We can be there, listen, really listen, and take seriously their concerns. On that afternoon I met Ethel, my motives were all wrong, but regardless, it turned out all right.

The Unacceptable Alternative: Divorce

Divorce is an ugly word and especially true in the church circles I frequented in the early 1970s. "You made your bed, now asleep in it" was an expression I heard back then about marriage. The idea of divorce when I married in 1953 never crossed my mind, because I was absolutely certain this would never happen, but after nineteen years, happen it did. I faced two alternatives, staying in a loveless marriage or divorcing. Both alternatives for me were unacceptable.

The details of the dissolution of my marriage are not unique. Back then if neither party contested the divorce, irresolvable conflicts were often the reason stated on divorce decrees. Even though in the church circles I frequented divorce was not acceptable, it was permitted in the case of adultery. The innocent party, the one offended against, was welcomed in the church, the other in many cases was shunned, cut off, left to his/her sinful ways. Our divorce was based on the grounds of irresolvable differences, however I was the one who filed. I was the first in my family to divorce and I was a minister.

Of course guilt stalked my life and I did feel shunned, cut off. How much of what I experienced was of my own making, my sense of shame and my own withdrawal and how much was actually rejection is difficult to determine.

I met June (not her real name) in a small group that Ann and I attended weekly. Small groups were just coming into the life of the church in the late 60s. This group consisted of four or five couples who deeply shared struggles and challenges. June was a part of this group, and it was to her that I fled when I left home. Having no money, she arranged for me to live with a male friend of hers who owned a mountain cabin about 18 miles from Denver.

As an evangelical Christian I always tried to do everything right. Raised in a Christian home, I accepted Jesus as my personal savior. I attended church regularly, attended a Christian college, married a Christian girl, pursued education at an evangelical seminary, became a conservative Baptist minister, loved Jesus seeking to put him first in my life—yes, even ahead of my family. I did everything supposedly all right only to see it turn out all wrong.

If that doesn't turn one's world spinning on its head I don't know what will. The woman to whose arms I fled to was not evil; she was kind, caring, nurturing, tender and loving. She became my salvation in escaping a marriage that I now believe should never have taken place in the first place. From that experience, which lasted only briefly, I learned to be less judgmental, more understanding of sexual sins, I learned something about compassion; and most importantly, I learned that God's grace is limitless. Apart from grace, I understand I am a doomed man.

I believe that what happens to us is not as important as what we learn from what happens to us. Learners make the same mistakes as non-learners, but after one or two trips down the wrong path they stop and turn around. That's repentance, an about face, going in a different direction. Non-learners just keep on doing the same thing expecting a different result. Learning is what life is all about; and if we are learners, learning continues until we die.

I wanted out of ministry, wanted nothing to do with the church or God and felt betrayed by both; I no longer knew what I believed if anything. I learned to dance and swear, and I experienced my one and only bout of drunkenness. I was having a midlife faith crisis rebellion.

Yet, I was a learner. I learned so much about compassion, loneliness, hurt and pain, self-righteousness, judgmentalism. I learned talking the talk was hollow and walking the walk difficult if not impossible.

For me at that time, in the middle of my crisis, there was also the question of how I was going to make a living if I was no longer a preacher. I considered selling used cars, but I was not a good salesman in my single days before marriage. I thought maybe I could be a chaplain in a hospital or mental health clinic or nursing home; I thought I could salvage my seminary degree that way.

I applied for a position as a hospital chaplain only to discover that my divorce was not what troubled my interviewer but the fact that I had no clinical pastoral education (CPE) training. Soon I discovered that there were a number of centers in the Denver area where ministers and seminary students could obtain CPE training.

A basic unit (or quarter of CPE) involved a full-time, intense experience, an inward journey. Through seminars and interactions with patients the focus in CPE was not on the patient but upon what the student was learning about himself/herself. Prior questions were explored. The common assumption is if you want to be a minister you attend seminary and train to be a minister; however, a prior question is "What makes you think you should be a minister?"

A basic unit of CPE excited me, and with a basic unit under my belt I would be eligible for employment as a chaplain in hospitals, mental health centers and other clinical settings. Of particular interest to me was the CPE program at Fort Logan Mental Health Center. So I applied, only to be turned down.

With persistence, I applied again for admission into the CPE program at Fort Logan. My conviction was if I were accepted in the program, I would receive a modest stipend, enough to cover my obligations for child support. This time I was accepted.

Years later, after taking nine quarters of CPE and becoming a certified supervisor of clinical pastoral education, my Fort Logan supervisor told me he initially turned me down because I came across as rigid, intense, uptight, and opinionated. He questioned whether or not I would be open to the inward journey and able to ask myself hard questions. He told me he accepted me for a basic unit because he needed a warm body, another student to conduct his program. I sure got a break.

I loved Fort Logan and my first sustained experience with professionals who were not evangelical Christians. The professionals on the mental health teams I rotated through accepted me. There was no judgment, no condemnation. I felt genuinely cared for and loved. I soaked up time spent with ministers from other denominations who were also in the CPE program.

I Meet My Miracle: Jackie

During a rotation through the geriatrics unit at Fort Logan I met Jackie. She was the head nurse on that unit. She was a beautiful woman who was single, having a similar experience as me with the failure of her first marriage. I wasted no time in writing a note to ask her out. Reluctantly, she accepted a dinner invitation. We hit it off and started dating on a regular basis, and I fell in love with her.

Jackie was clear with me that she did not want to marry a minister. As she was a private person, the idea of being the first lady in a church was unappealing. I assured her that it would not be a problem because I had no intention of every going back into parish ministry. I was destined to be a CPE supervisor within a CPE program in a local hospital or mental health center. She was not at all sure she wanted to marry a man with five children. I assured her their mother would never give them up, and the boys would soon be on their own.

When I fell in love with Jackie I liked that she was not raised in the church and rarely attended. She had little understanding of the evangelical world I spent my life in. Our values were similar regarding money, family, travel, pleasure, sex, and — strange as it might seem — even faith. In September 1973, we married under the weeping birch in the backyard of her Harvey Park home. The minister and two attendants were the only invited guests. Little did the two of us know that in a few years I would be the minister at St. James Presbyterian Church and she would share the responsibility of raising my children.

Jackie never really saw herself as a minister's wife. Not knowing how to play the role, she never tried. She never sang in the choir, served on a committee, taught Sunday school, or accepted an invitation to speak. She found it difficult even to sit as an honored guest at a church gathering. She simply attended church, seeking to sit wherever she so desired as any other parishioner. She liked being inconspicuous. She didn't attend because of her love for the church but because she happened to be in love with the man who pastored that church. She saw herself as the partner of a man who was a minister and who found love and acceptance in the church he served. She saw her job as that of listening, encouraging, and just loving her man. As long as he was happy, she showed no interest in changing his vocation. Many in the church did not know I was married or whom this lady named Jackie was.

When I was required to be at a church function she would ask, "Do you want me to come along?" If I answered no, for I knew she often did not want to come, I'd say, "It's okay if you stay at home." If I indicated that I wanted her to be by my side, she came lovingly and willingly.

Ironically, her low profile as a pastor's wife served her well. She was admired for not playing the traditional minister's wife role. She was applauded for being her own person, pursuing her own profession. Of course, there were those who were disappointed that she was not more visible, but she never allowed those voices to influence her.

Though not involved in the life of the church Jackie enthusiastically threw herself into the role of parenting five children. Jackie entered our marriage with a grown daughter of her own. Difficulty in the birthing of her daughter resulted in her not being able to bear additional children. Now, unexpectedly she found my five children an integral part of the family. I never detected that she resented the children; rather, with few exceptions, she delighted in them as a part of our lives.

The boys were older at this time and for the most part wanted to be on their own. They were slow to accept her as any other than their father's new wife, a woman they had no part in selecting. They were kind, and yet at times rebelled and made life difficult for her as normal teenagers do. The two girls immediately took to this new lady in their dad's life. Her kindness, gentle spirit, and caring nature were hard to resist, and Jodi, the youngest, called her mom from childhood days on.

It was not easy for Jackie because Ann had primary custody. Though the children spent a great deal of time with us and Ann did not object, she would not grant me custody. This created difficulty particularly when dealing with school officials. Still somehow Jackie made it work. When there was a school activity involving the children, our attendance was a priority. She loved my birth children as much as if they were her own, although the return of that love varied depending on the child. Jackie was a healer, an avoider of conflict if at all possible.

Ann had a difficult time accepting Jackie and did not attend family gatherings for many years after I married Jackie. At the dinner following the memorial service for our oldest son, John, who died in 2011, Jackie approached Ann, now known as Anna and said, "Anna, since we love the same people, you suppose we might be friends?" And the two became friends; not close friends, but friends. Anna started attending family gatherings when Jackie and I were present. The last time

Jackie was able to attend a family gathering prior to her death in 2015, Anna followed her to the door and said to her, "I love you Jackie." I still tear up when I think of the magnanimous nature of my lady, Jackie.

Part II

My Son Thomas

Chapter 5

From One World to Another

After Thomas came out of the closet, he entered a relationship with an older man, a rancher from Fort Collins with money. This relationship lasted for a while, then Thomas moved home. For the next few years his life looked back on track. At 22, he met and married a fine Christian lady named Terry. He held nothing back from Terry about his past. She knew of his homosexual life and his battle with drugs, but they both believed all of that was history.

Thomas and Terry grew in their Christian life. In time, two children were born, Ashleigh and Jennifer.

Thomas and his family moved to Fort Collins where they became active in a small fundamentalist church. Thomas craved the simple black-and-white answers such a church provided. Thomas consented that another should order his life, and the pastor of that little church was more than willing to do that. The minister invited Thomas to go to Albuquerque to be part of a church plant there. Though not ordained, his role was to be that of an unofficial assistant pastor in the new church. And so, Thomas loaded up the family's few earthly possessions in a U-Haul and set off for New Mexico.

Then one night the phone rang. "Dad, I need you. Can you come?" The voice on the other end of the line asked. It was Thomas, and there was no doubt that he was in trouble.

Tom met me at the airport, the picture of defeat. The homosexual feelings that he was so sure were gone forever returned with a vengeance. He gave into temptation and acted out. Feeling ashamed, he went to the pastor and confessed. The pastor's response was to immediately remove him from the church. Disowned and having no place to turn, Thomas determined to kill himself in such a way to make his death look like an accident so that his family might collect insurance. Before putting his plan into action he picked up the phone and called me. I think had I not gone, Thomas might have killed himself. He showed me the bridge abutment he intended to drive his car into at full speed.

Those few days in Albuquerque were heavy days, yet as we talked hope was reborn. He spoke of not wanting to lose his family and of his love for Terry. He felt awful about what he put her through. He spoke of wanting to be delivered from his homosexuality. I made inquiries among some friends and learned of a ministry called Exodus based in San Francisco, a ministry of deliverance for gays. Thomas contacted Exodus, and they invited him and his little family to come to California where they promised they would work with him, help him get settled and see him through this crisis. And so, together we packed a U-Haul trailer. With a heavy heart, I told them goodbye and watched as the little family headed west. Our hopes were in Exodus. Somehow deliverance would happen again; we just had to believe.

But deliverance didn't happen. The Exodus experience was a disappointment for Thomas. He soon drifted away from that organization and turned to Homosexuals Anonymous. During the next two years, Thomas attended HA meetings and ultimately moved into leadership. But all along, he confessed later, while leading meetings, his own homosexual feelings raged inside of him. Then, he began acting on those feelings. This time, the duplicity of his life brought him to the point of confession to Terry. They packed up their belongings one more time and headed back to Fort Collins to be near our family and Terry's.

Thomas found a job as a florist at a small floral shop. He did very well there, so well that after a few years the gentleman who owned the shop, wanting to retire, made it possible for Thomas to buy the business. Now Thomas decided he could not fight his homosexual feelings any longer and could not go on living a double life. He and Terry agreed to divorce. The very night he left home, Thomas made his way to a gay bar where he met Larry, and soon they were living together.

We talked frequently during this time. I told him on one occasion, "Thomas, do you understand? There is nothing you can do to make me love you less. There is nothing you can do to make me love you more. I just love you. What is at stake here is not my love for you. What is at stake is your life." With the AIDS epidemic in full swing, I was frightened for Thomas. I tried to brace myself for the reality that he might contract AIDS.

Whereas in the earlier years, I prayed that Thomas might be delivered and experience a normal, heterosexual life, now I no longer prayed that prayer. Now, I just prayed that somehow God would be there for Thomas. I once again let him go and relinquished him to the Lord. After all, by this time, Thomas was 35 years old. I knew that God cared more for Thomas than I did. God was the one who brought him into being. One thing I came to believe was if I as an earthly father could not stop loving my son how could God stop loving him? In my prayers, I would just hold up his name before the Lord and ask God to take care of him. Mostly, my prayer was, "Thy will be done."

Thomas and I clearly understood each other. He knew that I did not approve of his lifestyle, but he knew that he was loved and accepted. The more I understood of his lifestyle, the more I became aware of the loneliness and pain in the homosexual world. I suspect there are happy practicing homosexuals, but I am not sure I met any. In meeting many of Thomas' friends, I met deeply troubled and distressed men, desperate to be accepted and loved. They longed for instant deliverance from their pain and believed it could happen if they could just find the *right man*.

I find it rather ironic that the term *gay*, which when I grew up meant frivolity and fun, lighthearted and carefree has come to be associated with the homosexual world. I am not an expert on homosexuality, but Thomas and his friends were anything but lighthearted and carefree. Their lives revolved mostly around a homosexual bar in Fort Collins. What only became apparent later on was that Larry and Thomas' lives also revolved around the consumption of drugs: marijuana, cocaine, speed and crystal meth, and, of course, alcohol.

Thomas spoke of wanting a long-term relationship, but with a man, not a woman; and he believed Larry was this man. Now I wanted that for him, too—some kind of happiness. If he insisted on living his life with another man, then I wanted him to enjoy a faithful and loving relationship. Larry was a warm, likable guy who, along with Thomas, was welcome in our home and at family gatherings. He and Thomas would spend weekends with Thomas' daughters. On the occasions we would visit Thomas and Larry at their rented house in Fort Collins, I was aware of tension and at times division. Still both Thomas and Larry treated the girls with kindness. When they knew we were coming they did their best to show their tender side and to refrain from drugging for a few hours. When the girls were not there, the two continued to live a life marked by continual drug use.

Then, Thomas announced that he and Larry were going to be married. He wanted me to attend, but I could not bring myself to go to the bar where the unofficial wedding was to be held. So I was not there when the two *tied the knot* figuratively speaking.

It was ordained that Larry, also a floral designer, would work in the floral shop that Thomas now owned, but the floral shop business was declining as the pile of unpaid bills mounted. Thomas trusted Larry to do the bookkeeping and remained oblivious that the shop was going under. Much of the money that came in went up Thomas and Larry's noses as their addiction continued. There were physical fights. As Larry brought drugs home every night it was inevitable that their lives would fall apart. Unable to pay the loan taken out to buy the business, the former owner took foreclosure steps. Bankruptcy followed, and the floral shop in Fort Collins that was to be Tom's future was now history.

The predictable downward slide continued with more drugs, more alcohol and fighting. Then Thomas discovered that Larry was seeing other men. That was the final straw; and after seven years, the two parted.

My youngest son, Ned, and his wife, Kim, opened their home to Thomas and offered him a job. The first weekend, Ned invited Thomas to go with his family to the Home Show, and Thomas accepted. Ned was aware that he was restless that night. The car was no sooner parked, when Thomas announced he would not be going to the Home Show but rather to an AA meeting in downtown Denver, and he would catch a bus back to their home in Parker.

The phone rang at 2:00 a.m. the next morning. Thomas was desperate and could they come get him? He was at a sleazy motel on East Colfax, the skid row of Denver. Ned and Kim awakened friends who were able to watch their girls and headed for the motel. Thomas never intended to go to an AA meeting but rather to the nearest gay bar. On the way to the bar, he met a man, a total stranger, who proposed they get high and spend a few hours together in a motel. Thomas agreed.

They went to the motel and started drinking, and Thomas gave the stranger what little money he had for the purchase of drugs. The deal went sour, and Thomas was now drunk and out of money.

I was out of town on this particular weekend. Not knowing what to do, Kim called Jackie, and Jackie encouraged Ned and Kim to get Thomas into treatment. And so, the two of them awakened Thomas early the next morning and announced plans to take him to Arapahoe House, a treatment center for alcoholism and drug addiction. When I returned, I immediately found

Thomas. It was hard for me to see my son in such a setting—denial is something I am good at. He didn't belong there with the dregs of society. Not Thomas. But there he was, sleeping on a simple cot in a room filled with junkies of which he was one.

From Arapahoe House, Thomas was transferred to a treatment center in Commerce City where he stayed for a month. Unsuccessful attempts were made to get him into Sobriety House, a long-term treatment facility. When the 30 days were up at the Commerce City treatment center, Thomas was discharged. It wasn't practical for him to live with us in our mountain home. He had no way to get to work each day. So Jackie and I decided to aid him in renting his own apartment in the Capitol Hill area in downtown Denver. Thomas was determined to live in that area.

I picked him up at the treatment center, and we headed for the inner city. Thomas, now 41 years old, was still a charmer, sensitive, caring and articulate. I feared the city would devour him. My message to him was clear. We were invested in his sobriety. We were invested in him staying alive, not killing himself. We were not trying to get him to change his sexuality.

For several days Jackie helped Thomas search for a place to live. Thomas didn't have any money, and so Jackie put up the deposit and signed the lease. Thomas was always special to Jackie, and this woman who was a gift of God to me was also to Thomas. Jackie was the most generous person.

The apartment would not be available for several weeks, and so each night until he was able to move in, I drove Thomas down to AA meetings in the city. I sat in the car and waited for the meeting to be over and for him to return. He always chose to go strictly to homosexual recovery groups. I wondered if any of those men who walked through the doors might just be the happy homosexual I never met. This much seemed certain: they were troubled and in need of help.

The hour passed quickly, and afterwards Thomas and I talked. Mostly he would tell me whom he met at the meeting. I discover that Tom's motivation for going to the meeting was not just treatment but also a place to meet other homosexuals. Maybe there he would find a friend. He told me that a lot of guys gave him their phone numbers and an open invitation to call should he need to talk. While Thomas could quickly make friends and he enjoyed a steady parade of people throughout his life, none stayed very long.

The day we helped him move into his apartment, he introduced us to a new friend, a handsome man named Kevin. In his 30s, Kevin was dying of AIDS. To look at Kevin you would never know he had AIDS. Kevin appeared to be strong and healthy and insisted on helping Thomas move, but before we carried many boxes into the apartment I found him sitting on the front seat of his car, his head in his hands. "Are you all right?" I asked. He explained that he was out of energy and unable to help anymore.

I never saw Kevin again. A few months later, Thomas told me he died. He ultimately got an infection, and his body, unable to fight it off, succumbed. Almost all of Thomas' friends were sick. Relationships of necessity in Thomas' world seemed so casual and temporary.

Thomas wished to get involved with Metropolitan Community Church, and he attended on occasion, but religion was not a central part of his life anymore. He spoke of faith in God. He told me how so many people in the fundamental, evangelical churches told him he was going to hell unless he ceased being a homosexual. But he told me he knew they were wrong. He stated that you don't get to Heaven by what you do or don't do. "You get there because of what God has already done for you in Jesus. Grace," he said, "not damnation, was the final word. If you have to do something, anything, then salvation is really by works." It sounded like good theology to me.

Chapter 6

Will It Ever End?

Needing work, Thomas was thrilled to find employment at the Blue Moon Floral Shop. The owner, manager, almost every employee, was gay. They did not put Thomas on the payroll but instead paid him under the table. Each morning when someone from the shop went to pick up the flowers, that person also returned with drugs (mostly crystal meth) for everyone.

Now at Blue Moon, drugs became the main component of Thomas' life. By keeping him on speed, the shop owner could work him 14 to 16 hours a day. And when payday came around, there wasn't much to take home because the cost of the drugs was deducted from his salary.

During this time, my youngest daughter, Jodi, got married. Thomas agreed to make the floral arrangements for his sister's wedding. The night before the wedding, Thomas stayed up all night putting together the floral arrangements. He never made it to the service and only put in a brief appearance at the reception. The reason, we learned later, was that he was high on speed. He was "too wired to be around so many people."

Jackie and I prepared to leave on a trip to Florida to visit her family. The day before we departed, Thomas called. He was distraught. Can we come and get him, he asked. The day before his call he quit Blue Moon. The drugs finally caught up with him, and in a psychotic break, high on drugs, he ran out of the shop, screaming.

Thomas needed a treatment center, but Jackie and I were at a loss of where we might find one that would accept him. He was obviously dependent on drugs and alcohol. We picked him up and brought him to our mountain home. We knew we needed to cancel our Florida trip and place Thomas in treatment. The next morning, Jackie said to me, "I've been thinking. Let's take Thomas along with us to Florida. We'll enjoy three weeks with him, three weeks wherein he might dry out and some time to consider what our next step will be." What she suggested resonated with my spirit. I felt it an answer to prayer. And so, the three of us set out for Florida in our extended cab pickup truck pulling a fifth wheeler.

I was not prepared for those days spent with Thomas. At times, I was angry with him for the way he trashed his life. But I saw how frighteningly fragile he was, and I accepted how limited he was. The drugs had done a frightening number on him. I wondered to what degree drugs destroyed part of his brain. In the early days of the trip, Thomas was mostly silent. He was never sullen or belligerent. There was no meanness in Thomas. As the days passed, he became more verbal, and we enjoyed long, rich talks. I found myself feeling overwhelmingly sad. I once again allowed this son of mine into my heart, and I just wanted to sit and hold him and cry. I hurt for him and the pain he was so obviously in.

All Jackie and I could offer him was a normal life. A conversation over a cup of coffee, and evening at home with a good book, a walk, a shared meal; and I was not sure that normal was enough for Thomas. His life required the abnormal: drugs, alcohol, and sex. We could only offer him that which from his perspective felt boring, predictable, and normal.

He sat and journaled for hours stretched out in the back seat of the fifth wheeler. Sometimes he shared what he wrote. He was a delightful traveling companion, and when we arrived in Florida, he and I unhooked the fifth wheeler, jumped into the truck and headed for the Florida Keys—a father and son doing whatever for two days. We laughed and talked. We even laughed at the black humor of his chaotic life. We found a motel along the shores of the Keys and after a good meal settled in for the night. Once again, I let Thomas steal my heart. When I could distance him and stay somewhat angry with him I didn't experience this tender side toward him. Part of me resented what I was feeling because to feel so deeply hurt. The pain was acute, and I was tender.

I wondered how this son of mine—who even at 40 was just a boy—could make it in this world. I wasn't sure he would. They say that when you are addicted to drugs your emotional development often gets stunted at the age you first started using; I could see this happening to Thomas. At times, he acted like a teenager. He had beautiful ideas of what he wanted to do with his life when we returned to Colorado. Jackie and Thomas wanted to open a booth at the flea market. Thomas wanted to make all kinds of artsy things to sell in the booth. But like a teenager, he was unable to follow through on those ideas. They were just dreams as fleeting as the wind.

He loved the coast of Florida and enjoyed walking in the sand of Panama City Beach, but always—just beneath the surface—I was aware of a restlessness, an emptiness, a loneliness; and I knew I could do nothing about that. I wasn't able to fill the void or the emptiness he felt. Too soon, the Florida trip ended, and we were back in the real world, the familiar scenes of everyday life.

With a heavy heart, we parted and he returned to his apartment on Capitol Hill. Two nights later, the phone rang. Thomas asked if we would come and get him. Once again, he wanted to kill himself. "We will be there right away, Thomas," I said. "Please, don't call the police," he pleaded. I assured him we wouldn't, and we headed for the city. Reluctantly, he opened his apartment door. He had been drinking and smoking marijuana while writing suicide notes.

"No one can help me except God," Thomas said.

Since he believed that was true, he just wanted to die so he could be with Jesus. I didn't know how to respond to this. I told him I didn't want him to die, that I didn't know what I would do without him. I said that I knew his children would never get over it. Thomas could not absorb my words. At times, suicidal thoughts dominated his life more than drugs, all compelling, relentless. Never having experienced such thoughts and seeing life as a beautiful gift, I could not understand.

"Where are you going to take me?" he asked.

"We are going to take you where you can sober up," I responded. "Tomorrow, we will talk." And so, slowly he gathered his things together and we headed for the car. Silently, we drove along. There was nothing to say, only the heaviness, the incredible sadness and pain of the moment.

"I want you to take me to Denver General. I'm afraid I might kill myself if I come to your house." And so I turned the car around and we made our way to the emergency room. The starkness of reality was hard to deny.

When a female psychiatrist questioned Thomas he became very belligerent. "What do you mean, how can you help? You ought to know how you can help. I'm here to get help."

"Well, you are obviously drunk," she responded. "We won't talk to you now because it will only be the alcohol talking. Come back in the morning, and we will talk with you." My heart sank because I feared that Thomas might not be with us in the morning. All except one of his suicide attempts had occurred while under the influence of drugs and alcohol.

Thomas hesitated and said, "I am afraid of what I will do to myself if I go home with my mom and dad." Now we had the attention of the psychiatrist, and he was allowed to stay. The next day, I returned to Denver General. But there now was hope. Somehow, there was always hope or at least one had to hang on to the idea of hope. Maybe there would be some kind of deliverance or at least deliverance from drugs and alcohol. Two doctors took a deep interest in his case, one a psychiatrist and the other a psychologist. They agreed to meet with him weekly. An anti-depressant was prescribed to help him level off. We decided Thomas could live at a house we owned in the city, the Winona house, a house Jackie purchased before I met her and in which we were now living having sold our mountain home. We remodeled the house in anticipation of our golden years. Thomas liked the idea of living at that house. His lease was up on the downtown apartment, and Jackie and I helped him clean. He agreed that there would be no drugs or alcohol at the Winona house.

The weeks rolled by, and Thomas seemed to be adjusting well to living there. He kept his appointment with his doctors and AA meetings on occasion attended . He made new friends, and we found it promising that his new homosexual friends were not abusing drugs and alcohol. Jackie worked with him daily and was there for him whenever he wanted to talk.

He did some tasks around the house but lacked follow-through. Projects were started but not finished. He seemed oblivious of the obvious things that needed to be done. If you asked him to do something, he did so willingly, but there was little self-motivation. Mostly, he was self-absorbed, rarely asking questions about our lives. He talked about his children, who now at 13 and 15 were deeply concerned about his well-being. Jennifer, the 13-year-old, intuitively sensed when things were not going well for him. She wrote, "Daddy, I know you struggle and hurt, and I hurt for you. I would do most anything to help you. I would get on my bicycle and ride to Denver if I could just help you." Thomas spoke of his love for his girls, but it was apparent that they were not a priority in his life.

For a while, he held a job as a tree trimmer with a friend, his sponsor in AA, but one day, learning that his employer offered no workman's' compensation insurance, and on that same day feeling belittled and humiliated by his employer, he quit. He felt rejected because not only did he lose his job, he also lost his sponsor. His sponsor never contacted him after that. He confessed to Jackie that he used marijuana daily. He slipped out with regularity and sat in his battered Yugo to smoke pot.

For Mother's Day, he wrapped up his pot parapher- nalia and gave it to Jackie. I suspect few mothers ever received such a gift. He again was determined to get off drugs. He became more and more withdrawn, and I wondered — almost knowing — if he was using again.

Soon he asked if he could talk with me. He spoke of how he felt a need to rebel against me just because I was his father. I understood that. He needed to be inde- pendent, he said. I told him independence also meant financial independence and that was not happening. By this time, Thomas' addictions left him owing money to a number of people. He always intended to pay back what he owed, but somehow he never got around to doing so. The need for immediate gratification ruled his days and nights. His weakness in the face of addiction was apparent.

I became aware again how limited he was. Such limitations were not apparent upon meeting him. He was gracious and possessed abundant social skills. His doctors also became aware of his limitations. They are the ones who first realized that he could not work for any length of time so, they who urged him to apply for food stamps as well as aide for the disabled. I found it painful to accept that my son would become a ward of the state. Somehow, as we set out to help him complete the necessary paperwork, we needed to believe — as he needed to believe — that it was only temporary.

Once again, I sensed Thomas was pulling away from us and suspected he was using drugs and alcohol. And then came the night we almost lost him. Jackie was rest- less that night; she knew something was wrong. Sleep wouldn't come. Not known to us, at the Winona house,

Thomas sat in his room drinking and writing suicide notes. His plan was to drive to a remote place and ingest 160 pills. He was preparing to leave the house when someone knocked at the door. It was Stephen, a friend he hadn't seen in a while, a man he thought he was in love with. Stephen had never before come to the Winona house, but now he was at the door. Thomas saw Stephen's arrival as a divine intervention.

He told us of the desire to kill himself in the morning and reported to his doctors who wanted him to check in at Denver General for treatment. Hearing and assimilating the meaning of the word *addict* was difficult for him and us. The intensive program at Denver General would last for only a week. The goal would be to regulate his anti-depressant medication and start him on Antabuse. His doctors were concerned with his obsession with suicide. At times, he found himself far more obsessed with killing himself than with drugs. His depression was increasing in spite of the antidepressant he was taking. "I am an addict," he said.

Addict is such a stark word. My son was an addict. Addicts can't hold jobs for any length of time. They lack follow-through. They are fully narcissistic. Their world is a shrunken one focusing on when they can get their next fix. Thomas told us that the only time he feels good is when he is high. He said sober living is too frightening.

For a week, he wrestled with not wanting to go the hospital, but now as he talked with me, it became apparent that he was ready. And so, after stopping at the welfare office where he made the initial application for food stamps, I again drove him to Denver General Hospital. There, he found himself with a homosexual roommate in his early 20s who was blind and partially deaf. His blindness was the result of a botched suicide attempt. So much unhappiness, so much despair. As the week in Denver General drew to an end, once again we hoped Thomas might be accepted into Sobriety House, but Sobriety House refused to admit him because of his suicidal tendencies.

A few days later, Thomas told us that an old friend of his, a woman who worked at the Fort Collins flower shop, wanted him to spend a month with her and her family in California. At first, I felt this was more running away. But then I wondered if in some strange way something beautiful might happen in California. She would send him a round-trip ticket under the condition there would be no drugs or alcohol.

I was relieved when he arrived in California and felt ashamed that I was relieved. When he wasn't around we obviously weren't in control, not that we had ever really been. When Thomas was away, I found myself sleeping easier, but always beneath the surface there was the pain. That dull pain that nothing could take away. Maybe it will never go away, I thought.

At the time, I met weekly with good friends for support. During one meeting, they related the story of going to church and hearing the preacher put down gays. I found myself fighting the tears, feeling anew the pain that comes from loving a son whose life knows no deliverance. I suspect that many will say, "He brought it all on himself!" Much of what happened he brought on himself, but whether we cut ourselves or someone else cuts us, we bleed, and it hurts. And sometimes, I think that it hurts more when we bring it on ourselves, because the pain is compounded by guilt and self-contempt for our own stupidity. We know we are not victims. We made the wrong choices—choices we are now not at liberty to undo.

"What can we do to help?" someone asked in the group.

"What you have done by just listening has helped," I said. We are fixers at heart, and we want to take away the pain. The last thing we want to hear is that we may just need to live with it, maybe even until we die. We don't want to hear that it is okay to feel acute, relentless pain. At times it subsided as the miles separated us from Thomas. But it returned without warning when I allowed myself to feel — to feel love for my boy and to know that he in turn loved me. The men in the group gave me the gift of presence as they entered into my pain. And then they prayed for me and for Tom, and I was grateful.

Thomas' drinking and drugging continued for the next five years as he spent nights in gay bars, sometimes seeking sex with men whose names he did not know. He secured a temporary job in a floral shop and was no longer living with us. Calling yet once again drunk and threatening suicide, Jackie and I, along with his sister Jennifer went to him. Drunk and sobbing with alcohol speaking, we with troubled souls left him.

Shortly after that he hit bottom. He desired to be committed to the mental health hospital in Pueblo. With his consent we set up a meeting with a judge who granted him a forced 90-day commitment. The judge told him the only catch was that there were no current openings. The judge asked if possibly Thomas might stay with us temporarily. We agreed but Thomas told the judge it would not work; he knew where the closest bar was. Rather than coming to live with us because of his fear of continuing to drink, Thomas chose to spend two weeks at Denver Cares, a place where drunks who are rounded up on the streets of Denver are taken, hosed off, given a night's sleep and sent out in the morning. I visited him every day at Denver Cares, marveling at his determination to somehow overcome his addictions this time.

Thomas' time in Pueblo was a relief for us. We knew for 90 days the phone would not ring. But then he was released, and once again, he was back in our lives.

The next five years were a blur, one drunken episode after another, homelessness, living on the streets of Denver. Some things we remember vividly. While staying in a flophouse where he managed to get lodging, he turned on the gas stove without lighting the burners, hoping he would be dead by morning. Fortunately, a window above the stove was not sealed properly, and most of the gas escaped.

In 2000, his life changed radically. Thomas escaped from his latest lover's home where he was raped repeatedly and held prisoner. On a Sunday morning, unbeknownst to me, while I preached in a downtown church only two blocks away from his desperate barefoot flight in the snow, he ran toward Denver General Hospital. Once again he was admitted and released. Back at his miserable inter-city room he began watching Christian television. There he declared a miracle happened. He sensed God's presence and yet again gave his life to Christ. For three weeks he came home from his job as a floral designer at Newberry Florists in Cherry Creek drank, got high, and watched Christian television. For all of that in a way I still do not understand, his life changed, and from that day until his death in February 2015, he sought to serve Christ. Our God moves in strange ways, his wonders to perform.

The last three years of his life, Thomas suffered from an undiagnosed neurological disorder that left him stuttering, head jerking and wheelchair bound. Still he established what he called his mustard seed ministry to the homeless. From his small condo in downtown Denver he set out several days a week with sandwiches and copies of his testimony.

Unable to work for the two years prior to his death, he spent hours each day writing and journaling, completing 80-plus journals. Our time as father and son was rich and so rewarding during those last years as I drove him to secure food and medicine. We met with some regularity to dine and share our lives with one another.

Only after his death did I learn in reading his journals that he continued to occasionally binge drink. Ashamed, he did not want me to know. That he felt he needed to hide that reality from me saddens me. I wanted to believe that Thomas and I shared everything, but we didn't. I'm at peace with the truth that there are things your children don't discuss with you, and maybe that is the way it should be.

I've also come to know that life is about the journey. We were so destination-oriented growing up. Thomas' focus was not on the journey, but upon arrival.

I learned that if you travel well, the destination will take care of itself, and your days will expose you to many beautiful things along the way.

Chapter 7

The Writings of Thomas Avery

"The greatest thing you'll ever learn is just to love and be loved in return." – Thomas Avery

The call came at 2:15 a.m. on Valentine's Day, 2015. I was surprised because we were retired, and that was early for us to get a call. It was Daniel, Thomas' roommate, and he was in distress. "Thomas is on the floor and unresponsive!"

"Hang up and call 911," I said.

Jackie and I arrived at the hospital, and with dread asked for Thomas Avery. The receptionist said, "We don't have anyone here by that name." More dread. The hospital security guards came out and asked us to follow them to a small room where doctors joined us. "Your son has expired," they told us.

I thought, *Thomas is dead. Expired* doesn't soften the reality. *Passed away* doesn't help either. Passed away to where? My boy is dead, and no attempts to soften that reality will work. "I've got to see him," I said.

I was escorted to a room where he was laid out. There he was, but it was not Thomas. His body was hardly recognizable for all sorts of wires and tubes jetted out. He was not here. All that was here was the worn-out body that housed him for 59 years.

On Thursday of that same week, we held the memorial service. I was stunned when I arrived at the sanctuary of St. James Church where I served as a pastor for 22 years. Tom's daughters had set up tables with his poetry and writings on them. Off to the side was his favorite chair where he sat every morning, sometimes for six or more hours writing and praying—for him the best hours of his day. Next to the chair was a side table, and on the table his glasses.

The service was moving as some of his poetry was read. Thomas was described as a loving father, a deeply grateful son, an appreciative brother, a talented florist, a friend to the poor and homeless, vulnerable, and emotionally tender, physically weak and a mystic, a man whose love for God sometimes overwhelmed him and whose fear of God sometimes terrified him. As I listened I acknowledged that my boy fit all those descriptions. He was also open, honest, vulnerable and real. He was a man who—for all his sordid life journey—loved Jesus.

Here is a poem read at his memorial service. He called it "My Rebirth into Eternity."

Lord I am slain, yet I still am not free. Torrents of rain with dark wings envelope my body within, yet I am saved everyday all by your marvelous grace that consumes me in the end.

Where am I Lord, and who should I be? My tender heart longs for you even as I seek for meaning amongst the nails and the thorns that you lift me into the heavens, for one day I know I will be free.

Your love is soft and warm, refreshing my thirsty soul even as I look to see my rebirth into eternity. Your stars fall in love and burst into rays of light. With praise and adoration to you my Jesus, my heavenly Lord and King.

I looked at the picture of Thomas, which was taken when he was whole and healthy that is on the cover of the bulletin, and beneath it I read these words:

Thomas Peter Avery
September 23, 1955 – February 14, 2015

"I have lived one hundred lifetimes
and if it wasn't for Jesus,
I would have died one hundred score.
By his death I shall live forever more."
— Thomas Avery

I sat there trying to take it all in. The tributes were touching. His struggles with drugs and alcohol and homosexuality were addressed.

I know Thomas and I shared life deeply. I thought there was nothing he wasn't willing to share with me and how honored I felt that he was willing to do that. Sometimes he gave too much information, talked of things I just as soon would like to not hear about. Still I was deeply troubled for there was one thing he would not share with me and only after his death did I discover it.

Just a few days before he died I took him to the clinic to get some meds. We visited and he appeared fine, as okay as a man who dealt with headshakes, stuttering, a man who could barely walk, a man who was wheel chair bound could be.

What I learned from Daniel, his roommate, was on that very day, just prior to my picking him up, he had suffered a heart attack. He didn't want me or anyone else to know for fear we would insist on taking him to the hospital, and he was determined to never go to a hospital again. His life found him in and out of hospitals, and now he just wanted to die. Thomas was right, had I known I would have insisted on hospitalizing him. He knew that, and so he did not share with me the fact of his heart attack. It was just a few days later, on Valentine's Day 2015, that he instantly dropped dead of a massive heart attack. I was not prepared to let him go, but there was no doubt about it, Thomas wanted to die. He was ready for Heaven.

The day before he died he penned in his journal a poem by Saint Teresa of Lisieux, a little-known Catholic nun.

What I will soon see for the first time – I am still on the other shore, but sensing eternal happiness –

O I would already like to leave this earth and gaze on the wonders of heaven. When I dream of the joys of the other life, I no longer feel the weight of my exile, since toward my own home land I'll fly for the first time.

O Jesus give me white wings that I may take flight to you. I want to fly to the eternal shores, I want to see you, O my divine treasure, my beloved, let me soon

catch a glimpse of the sweetness of your first smile
and let me in divine delirium

Ah let me hide in your heart — O what a moment,
what ineffable happiness when I'll hear at the sweet
sound of your voice — when I see divine brilliance of
your adorable face for the first time

In his last years, Thomas wavered in his writings between seeing himself as despicable and claiming God's acceptance of him; he died wondering if God was punishing him for his sinful life by leaving him wheelchair bound, while at the same time celebrating God's love for him and the majesty of God's grace. He wavered between feeling so low, so undeserving that God could not forgive him, and so high that in ecstasy he bathed in God's love for the likes of him. Yet, I got the impression that he could never fully embrace that God's grace was unmerited favor, getting what he don't deserve.

There is something so sad about his life. Not because he was gay, but that except for brief moments, he never found the peace he longed for. Four themes emerge over and over again in the more than 80 journals Thomas left when he died: his love for the homeless and downtrodden, his unworthiness, His love for Jesus, and his homosexuality. I chose the following writings from his journals because they exemplify the four themes.

Thomas took great joy in making a half dozen peanut butter sandwiches and copies of his testimony and setting out in his electric chair to tour 16th Street in downtown Denver in search of homeless people. He prayed that God would lead him to the most needy. Upon encountering a homeless person, Thomas gave them a sandwich and a copy of a poem he wrote.

"A Street Blessing"

To all dear ones who have not a home,
May the concrete hard, be soft on your weary feet
May you find shelter each night that you may seek
May others never harm nor malign
May you fly high above each and every time
May you have warm clothing for each
    foreboding storm
May you have peace in your heart when you feel
    forlorn
May Christ's spirit rest deep inside your heart
May your destiny of hope be clear — each and
    every start
May you never lose faith upon each waking day
May you know God's love in the midst of dismay
May you find your residence in God's holy name
May you always feel welcome and know you're
    never alone
May God's word and truth live deep inside
May you never stray from Him, may you never
    ever hide
May the food you seek be from Heaven above,
    heavenly manna to feed with God's
    providing love.

Then along with "A Street Blessing," Thomas handed
them a copy of his testimony, which read like this:

> *I know where you are, I know where you've been,*
> *for I too have been homeless. I have walked these*
> *mean streets, alone, tired and weary. In hopes these*
> *words will find warmth in your heart, that you may*
> *continue to believe or start to believe and never give*
> *up. It is God who can give you your heart's desire.*

This is the way that one finds wealth in poverty, joy in sorrow, strength in meekness, satisfaction, grace in mercy, humility in the midst of war and joy in the morning.

This is the truth in the paradox of Jesus Christ. This is the very heart of melody and song. This is the beauty God gives in the ashes. Without it, the music of life loses its luster with no lasting beauty. Yet only God can manifest these virtues in us; for on our own, we cannot.

There was no question this addict's life was transformed. His writing was passionate, at times profound, and I was deeply moved by the genuine reality of his transformation.

Thomas' care for the downtrodden was seen in his love for Daniel, a homeless man. Though his small home at 18th and Pearl covered only 800 square feet, the two shared the space. When Thomas got sick, Daniel cooked for him and walked the dog while Thomas monitored Daniel's medications. One of his journals included this poem written about Daniel.

"The Most Beautiful Man in the World"
by Thomas Avery

The most beautiful man in the world is quite
        a sight to see
His statue so great, he stands six foot three
And everyone stops and stares to look at him
For he walks like Frankenstein, his feet turned in.
The most beautiful man in the world
Everything he does, he does with great care

He moves as slow as a turtle – obsessive compulsion
   to see
Except when he runs and his feet get the best of him
Raised eyes to glare and call him a freak
The most beautiful man in the world
He has a skin disease and wears long pants
   and sleeves
To cover his shame from those who would not
   understand, judging him
Even though he has a thyroid condition and
   overheats
His body melts on hot days to tear his heart within
The most beautiful man in the world
He cannot work because he can't get enough speed
The smallest task to please an employer waiting
Paychecks are for those who are able
A simple job to feel good about himself
The most beautiful man in the world
He can't drive a car just to get away
He can't swim far from his dismay, land bound,
   he walks everywhere
Amongst the stares
Cruel buses that don't care in the big, bad city he
   lives in
The most beautiful man in the world
His teeth are bad, but there's not much smiling
But he lights up when his funny bone is tickled
That's the stuff life is made of
Laughter from a big ball of love
The most beautiful man in the world
Autism is bound in a soul that can't get off the
   ground
Gentle spirit of another world – another land
No one understands the child trapped in the body
   of a man

Mysterious one who has no friends
The most beautiful man in the world
Reading a book is hard to digest
Dyslexic mind gets twisted in his head
So he cuts out pictures and words to sooth his world
That makes sense with his scissors to choose
The most beautiful man in the world
Communication is so very hard so he just
remains silent
But no one talks to him anyway except for his dog
and cat and roommate to lay
As if he doesn't exist, just a ghost in everyone's
imagination
But he thinks and hears and cares for those without
the patience
The most beautiful man in the world
His family wants nothing to do with him
Haven't talked with him in years
Last few times he was hospitalized his own mother
would not call him — even though I asked her
in tears
The most beautiful man in the world
World filled with sights and sounds we cannot hear
He lives on planes we cannot bear
Pills for schizophrenia help him to keep his feet on
the ground
Medications to numb the pain for a heart so rare
The most beautiful man in the world
The most beautiful man on earth has something we
don't, for you see, he has a heart of gold
As God has made him special such is his cross
to bear
The shining precious metal of his soul was made
for him who has eyes to see his beauty — hidden
beneath his extremities buried skin deep

The most beautiful man in the world was created for
you. Jesus created for God who deeply cares

Thomas' struggles with his own self-image are revealed in the following three journal entries.

And to the crux of the matter
In my wounded heart to reveal
As best I can
To feel – as though you, my God
Are not safe
As in disillusionment sorrow
Upon times of such seeking
To know and to prove
Your will to me – for my life to fulfill
Your greater fullness within
In shattered dreams
Upon the shards of glass
In my mirrors cracks
So I crawl on my knees
With new hope
Not my mother by my side
In healing for us
Not Church in the City to extend
a hand unto me
Yet for this final group
I am prepared
To commit myself to them
And you, my Jesus, sweet Jesus
As it seems to be
Preconceived ideas of what life should be
That tears me down most
My musical not
Is this life that I live

(2002) "Untitled" by Thomas Avery

Tears flow into empty hearts denied
and I live much as a loner
That cannot be denied
Too many wounds over years to atone for
Too many scars that live deep in my heart.
Is there a place for a hermit in seclusion?
Given a heart that longs for union
Heaven and earth in glorious fusion
But I can't break through to the other side
Though words woo and spill, they only tease
My heart denied, longing for Thee
I live my days as a lover in wait
Looking for one single touch to take me away
Into the heart of God
I am not a waste of space
As only things I have to give, I give away
Industry looked books unread
But for you, my Lord, as they are meant
For your eyes only
You are the incentive behind inky words written
You are my song, and I'll sing again
For into your heart I belong
You are my encouragement when words go wrong
And I've nothing left to give
But scribbling messages to my Beloved
Who is my inspiration all along?

(2012) "Lifeboat" by Thomas Avery

Stranded in waves of tempest,
lost at sea.
With no land to be seen
And only do they see one another
In differences to glare in accusing fashion.

Who should be thrown off the edge of humanity
As sustained life will not exist
In a lifeboat so small
With hungry mouths to feed
And too much weight
As to weigh down heavy
Upon the ocean of humanity
That holds them not
To value and compare each other's worth.

And what if one were a Christian
And one a Muslim
And one was gay
And another a witch

Their positions in life irrelevant
As the only thing each could see
Was glaring differences
Of humanity and faith
Or faith not
What to do and who to throw overboard
In order that
The majority survives
And all not perish?

The Christian prayed
And said to himself
I am God's chosen
A light and a beacon
To the lost souls in humanity
Surely it must be me
Who will be chosen by my peers
In order to save.

But they said to themselves
In judgment do you stand
With no love or acceptance to see me.
The witch and the Muslim
And gay one indeed to throw overboard
All your life constantly

And the Muslim prayed
Against the infidels he knew
Hated him so
As 9-11 did prove
That he with his race
Was out to overthrow
All on the boat — was it not true?

But they said to themselves
In fear do we hold you
In arms length to dread
What you think of us all
As we know that you wish
All of us dead.

And the gay one feared to pray
>*To a god or gods in his wake*
>*Whom he knew could overtake*
>*The waves of humanity*
>*To crush his soul*
>*To judge him so*
>*And call him less than human*

And he knew deep inside
>*That he could not hide*
>*From God's wrath*
>*And of theirs*
>*As dispensable was he*
>*And was always taught that he*
>*Was beneath all dignity.*

But they said to themselves
>*It is glorious we see*
>*Who should be sacrificed today*
>*For what good is this life*
>*That will not reproduce*
>*In flagrant display*
>*In our face*
>*We have seen him stand*
>*With equal rights to preach*
>*And shake our hand.*
I think not
>*As where has that hand been?*

And the witch sat back
  His soul to burn
  Upon stakes of humanity lost
  To burn
  To burn

What be the difference now
  To throw overboard – or burn

New stakes did he see
  Of his life as he
  Did offer spells and incantations
  Oh so silently
  To a god he knew not,
  But to the powers did he offer up
  Help on S.O.S. to save
  His soul instead

Of theirs on that boat
  To float, to float
  On the waves of humanity
  To decide which life
  Is expendable indeed

But they said to themselves
  A witch
  An abomination
  No respect does he show
  To a God we believe in
  Or a god we believe not
  Yet godless is he
  And deserves to be
  Burned at the stake
  In the waves of humanity.

And what if Jesus
          Was on that lifeboat
          And for whatever reason was his
          Decided not to speak
          As he so often did

Instead in silence did he sway
          Upon the waves of humanity
          Only to see
          Others to view him as different
          Than they

In homeless apparel would
          He portray himself
          Of what worth
          Would he be seen
          By others indeed
          To overthrow him
          It would seem
          Be the best
          As no home had he

And what if
          One man, or woman
          On that lifeboat at sea
          Tossed amongst the waves
          Of humanity
          Was terribly disfigured
          What we might call ugly
          As the hunch-back of Notre Dame
          Not easy to look at
          As we want to see
          What is pleasing to our eye

Then would it be true
> *That no matter who he was*
> *A gay man*
> *A Muslim*
> *A Christian or a witch*
> *That man would surely be*
> *On the top of everyone's list*
> *As unnecessary indeed*

One more mouth to feed
> *A waste of humanity*
> *And wouldn't we be generous to him*
> *In order to put him out of his*
> *Misery?*

That he must so live in
> *An act of mercy*
> *Would it truly be*
> *To throw him overboard*
> *And just set him free?*

But is it not true
> *That the gay man could be*
> *Also*
> *A Christian*
> *Or a witch*
> *Or a Muslim indeed?*

To hide inside in fear of his life
> *As his only friend could be*
> *The witch*
> *And of course Christ.*

No wonder the gay man
        Is caught up so
        In promiscuity
        As of you were told
        All your life
        That the end result
        Would be

No matter what you believed
Or did on this earth
Only hell to see.
Why not give yourself up
        To promiscuity
        To feel good for a season
        As eternity you'll spend
        In separation from God?
It's all so hard to comprehend

Thomas wavered between being unable to forgive himself for what he regarded as his wasted life, and being so loved by Jesus. In reading his journals I came across the following entry that tore at my heart. It never crossed my mind that anyone would be homeless in Heaven. How painful it must have been for my son to write the following.

"Homeless in Heaven" by Thomas Avery

Oh Lord, my heart is heavy and is set upon the
        gravity,
That weighs me down; so low I eat the dust of the
        ground;
Even as I hear church bells ringing in the distance
        clearly,

Death calls me closer, with each holy bell
that sounds.
This death that plunges daggers in my heart within
its attack
Calls me unto itself that I may know for certain,
I'm dying;
Even as life calls me unto herself, for she wants
me back;
But the bells that clearly ring are a portent of
all my sighing.

The hours tick away even as the hourglass pours its
sand
And I wonder about the midnight hour's ominous
ring
Calling me to itself, as time for me will soon no
longer stand,
For I can feel death with its icy hands around my
heart clutching
And I am not worthy of this life on Mother Nature's
earth;
And I am not fit for heaven, although I call it my
home!
This second birth rises above the death to show me
my worth
But I dream I will be homeless in heaven and
oh so alone!

An example has been laid, far from heaven's gate
Where I lie in anguish – all of my sins that I reap
now;
For when your books are opened, my name will be
last for the choices I made
Yet this soul that seeks solace of death will rejoice
somehow!

119

This world has blinded me, and now all pleasures
elude my senses;
And I, through all of this suffering, find only
pleasure in You, Lord!
I have given up and given into the church bells that
ring and lay down my defenses.
Deaths door knocks, even as my spirit pleads for life
a little more!

Your light, oh God, shines upon all the darkness of
this wasted life;
As all the shadows shrink into the darkness of
cockroaches;
And I am so sick that death cuts me in two with its
deadly knife;
Yet within each heart attack that strikes,
your will only encroaches.

I will not shrink from this pain that binds and
constricts;
And I will not fight the death that calls me home,
For even when I'm homeless in heaven,
if God sees fit,
He will be there with me, and I will not be alone!

For I'd rather be homeless in heaven than in the
hottest fiery hell.
And I will call myself blessed, for you, oh God,
have taken pity.
I know when I die, without a home in heaven,
I will be well
For heaven's abundance of glorious fruits will feed
me outside your holy city.

*I am not fit for your city, as the holy clothing I shall
    wear will be the most gorgeous garment I have
    ever worn
But not bright enough for all the stunning city
    garments to compare.
So I will make my home amongst your tender lilies
    and green grasses without any thorns.*

*So death, come what may
Your reaping will only produce joy
For God has forgiven all my great and terrible sins
And in his heaven will I finally have all the freedom
    to enjoy!
And even if I'm homeless in heaven, deep in my
    heart, I know that's when life begins!*

I am troubled when I read "Homeless in Heaven."
Troubled because my boy's self image was so shot that
he believed he would make it into Heaven but barely.
Maybe he thought he would live under a heavenly
bridge. Did he feel that God's grace abandoned him as
he wrote this poem? He mentions forgiveness of all his
sins but seemed incapable of internalizing the forgiveness. That deeply troubles me.

After his death, we discovered in the storeroom at
his condominium cases of bottled water and numerous
packages of dried food. The state of the world troubled
Thomas deeply, and he was convinced that Armageddon
would soon descend. He wanted to be ready. He
obsessed, and, yes, lived in fear that end times were
around the bend and believed he needed to be ready.
My gay son was so in love with Jesus and yet so fearful
of life, a complicated mix like the rest of us, a struggler
who soared high with the angels and also tumbled so
low that demons at times stalked him.

My journey with my beautiful son Thomas has led me from condemnation to homophobia, to toleration, to acceptance without approval, and finally to approval. I believe the predominant evidence is that homosexuality is genetic.

"Dad, when did you choose your sexuality?" he asked. I never considered such a question and responded somewhat defensively.

"I didn't choose it, I have always been attracted to women."

"And why would you think I would choose to be gay?" he replied. "Why would I choose rejection by the church, scorn and being called names by others?"

Reflecting I reminded myself that he fought his urges by marrying, believing that would eliminate any attraction to men. It did not. Ultimately, he gave into the homosexual lifestyle, abandoning any attempt to be straight. He acted out for years in a sinful way with multiple partners, one-night stands; this acting out was accompanied by drugs and alcohol. In the end, he lived as a celibate, struggling gay man, seeing himself as not fully accepted in the evangelical church.

Part III

God's Mysterious Ways

Chapter 8

Jackie – The Unexpected Paradox

God but I hate conflict. A friend of mine thrives on it. Once another man in our building called him an S.O.B., and I thought the two would duke it out. Fists clinched, faces red, neck veins popped out.

"Cool it!" I demanded, and they did, but I got the strange feeling that I messed with something the two were enjoying. I am sure there are people who thrive on the fight, but I am not one of them.

At times when I take a hard look I see my avoidance of conflict as cowardliness, weakness, and I judge myself as a pansy, a pushover. There have been those in my life who intuit my weakness and consciously or otherwise take advantage of it. A critical word, a disagreement, sharp words and my life goes into a tailspin. I obsess. The sun may be shining, but the day goes gray. I can't sleep as the scene plays over and over in my head.

Maybe Jackie and I got along so beautifully because we both hated conflict. Maybe our life together wasn't really as good as I wanted to believe. Was the idea that we had this special kind of love, where we rarely fought like other couples, just my imagination? The question emerges because other members of the family are sure they understood her better than I did, understood what her real desires were, knew what she really believed. They suggest that even though I lived with her for almost 43 years, I didn't truly know what she wanted or believed, and I am devastated.

My first marriage was not all bad, but over time, pettiness, selfishness, bitterness, and conflict exerted its ugly head, and the distancing began. We forgot how to nurture one another; we forgot tenderness; and we forgot how to love. Life became perfunctory, simply a matter of going through the motions year in and year out. Then angry words were spoken and divorce was imminent. (I think a lot of Christian couples live out their lives emotionally divorced. They end up just two people living together—day in and day out—in the same approximate space. They are in reality divorced; they just never have legitimized their divorce.)

Then, though uninvited, along came another woman who was affirming and nurturing and who saw the good in me, and my head spun. When I met June, the woman I went to after I left Ann, it was as if in the middle of a desert suddenly there was this well that I did not know existed; she was the well, and I could not drink enough of the life-giving water that poured forth from her.

I didn't wake up one day and say to myself, *This is a great day to go out and have an affair.* No, I am not saying it just happened, the seeds were sown years before when I thought I was doing right by putting God ahead of my family.

I yearned for someone to know my worth, but as we quarreled I began to believe the derogatory words Ann said about me even as Ann began to believe the derogatory words I said about her. If you stay in a sick relationship long enough you get sick. Once she was asked if there was anything good she saw in me, and her response was: "If there is I can't think of it." I know she was angry and striking out, but now 50 years later, it still stings as I recall. Don't tell me that words can't hurt you. Words hold the power to devastate. You see, always lurking is the question: Supposing what is being said is true?

The longing to be liked, the pain felt from rejection are driving forces. So when I met the woman of my dreams, not the woman I ran to after I left my wife, but my Jackie, and she—like me—knew the pain of rejection, the hurt of being unwanted, we fit. Together both of us just wanted to be nurtured. And so, throughout the next 43 years that is what we did. We nurtured each other, we loved each other; we drank deeply of that desert well that we stumbled into with an unquenchable thirst.

Now she is gone, and where shall that nurture come from? Did we—in our need to please—offer each other fool's gold? Some might think that it was a marriage too good to be true. If it was all an illusion, please don't peel the film from my eyes. Let me live believing.

There are those who say no marriages are made in Heaven, and I would number myself as one of them. Yet, the life I lived out with my Jackie was, as I saw it, a marriage made very close to Heaven. Maybe what counts is not how other people saw it. Let them think what they may. It is how I experienced my lady that I choose to think matters.

Jackie was an amazing woman who called forth the best in me, always cheering me on. She never left me doubting her love for me. Oh yes, there was that one time when after a bitter exchange, she said, "Les Avery, you can go right straight to hell!" but I knew she didn't mean it and within a few minutes we were back in each other's arms.

Am I easy to live with? Sometimes I am, and sometimes I'm not, just like everybody else. I am not rewriting history as some of my friends have done once their spouse is gone. You know what I mean. The departed was just wonderful, the perfect wife, . . . yawn, yawn. The truth was the marriage was a mess.

Jackie was the real thing, and I am the real thing. Perhaps hating conflict was the best thing going for us. We proclaimed our love for each other every day and tried desperately to live out the love we proclaimed. Were we unaware of each other's faults and limitations? Of course we weren't! It drove her nuts that I was never ready at the end of a church service when she felt it was time to go. As a pastor, I believed I needed to mix after a church gathering, and Jackie just wanted to go home. So there were the times I had her climbing the walls, but we mostly just accepted the need in the other person to do that which one or the other would rather they not do.

"I love you," I'd say.

"Right back at you," she'd reply. I saw no need to get all touchy feely every time I left the house, but for Jackie, it was essential that she accompany me to the door and give me a kiss. She knew how it felt to be abandoned, and I did everything in my power not to ever leave her feeling so.

When I did come in, no matter how late it was, she'd ask me if I was up to telling her about my day. Each morning I loved bringing her a cup of coffee, sitting with her, reading *Dear Amy* and then discussing whether we agreed with the columnist's advice.

It irritated me when in the middle of a deep conversation as we rode along in the car she would say (out of the blue), "Oh, look at that cow," or "That is a funny-looking barn over there?" Saying something randomly that had nothing to do with what I was talking about. It was her way of saying, "Shut up! I get it! Enough!" It took me a while to catch on.

"Where did that come from?" I would say. Her response was to just keep on looking out the window or to change the subject.

She spoke out every now and then with the wisdom of a philosopher. One day she said, "Les, would you rather be right or kind?" My response was I want to be both right and kind. She was aware that my tendency to be right often trumped being kind. My Jackie always chose kindness. You could say she chickened out, that she was fearful of conflict so she stuffed things down, and you would be right. She did stuff a lot of things down, often leaving the other person feeling she agreed with them even when she didn't. Criticize her if you like, and sometimes I did.

"Stand up for yourself," I said." She looked at me as if to say, "Look who's talking, as if you are the expert in saying it like it is." My Jackie would go out of her way not to offend.

Held by a magnet on the refrigerator was this quote: "In the resolving of conflict, seek not to offend rather than to be offended." Next to that one: "Seek to resolve the conflict, not to gain the advantage." Over and over again when faced with a family issue, I read those words, not that the mantra always worked. I suppose primarily because, like her, I wanted to avoid conflict if possible at all costs. We weren't fighters; we were lovers.

Suffering, that was something entirely different. Jackie knew how to suffer and suffer she did. Physical suffering plagued her for much of her life and particularly during her final years. High blood pressure, arthritis, sleep apnea, stomach cramps — you name it and she suffered from it, but she rarely complained. Some family members saw her as a complainer, but I never did which proves we experience people differently. I think both she and I suffered the most over unresolved family issues. At times in family gatherings there was the perpetual elephant in the room. You could feel the tension, but we avoided addressing the issue for fear of a blow-up. Yes, over the years blow-ups happened which only reinforced our determination to avoid conflict with others and with each other. She and I found inner pain harder to deal with than physical pain.

We loved to please each other and to defer to the other. It wasn't what movie or restaurant or motel that mattered, what mattered was whom we were with, and being with each other never grew old. The older we got, the less we wanted to quarrel with each other about much of anything. Just being together was enough.

If God tapped me on the shoulder on the day we married and said, "You go ahead and marry her, but know this, I am only going to give you 25 years together," I would have signed on in a heartbeat. Little did I dream that we would be granted for all our struggles almost 43 years of a married life beyond my wildest imagination.

I loved the fact that she was always young at heart, inwardly she never aged. No matter her age, to me she was always beautiful, sexy, sensual. To the very end, that holding power left me longing to lie with her, to hold her, to love her. We understood through the years of growing old the meaning of God's statement in Genesis, "The two became one flesh."

Dealing with the Inevitable

Several years ago my lady was diagnosed with liver cancer. The doctors told us surgery was the answer, and I wanted her to schedule going under the knife the next day, but others views wisely prevailed. The decision was not mine to make; it was hers. Like other areas in her life reluctance to decide drove me wild. I'm impulsive. If it needs being done, let's do it. Why wait? Jackie wasn't wired that way.

When I would accompany her into a dress store, she would say to me, "I like this one," and hold a dress on a hanger next to her body. I'd respond, "If you like it, let's get it."

"Let me think about it," she'd say.

"Jackie, what is there to think about? You want it, so let's get it!"

My insistence irritated her. Later, I learned that she returned to the store sometimes two or three times, always without me to check out the item. Sometimes she bought; sometimes not. For her, joy came from the hunt, in the shopping and desiring, wondering if the item would still be there. She did not like me to shop with her. A visit to a grocery store for her was a sensual experience to be treasured. Having picked up the items we came to buy, I waited at the register irritated and impatient until she showed up.

Finally, almost six weeks later, the surgery was scheduled. Even on the day of the surgery, my lady wondered if she should go through with it. Afterwards, eager to go home, she fought staying in the hospital. Getting well was not a priority with her because she saw herself as well. Still needing around-the-clock care, I found my joy spending nights with her at the hospital. After too-short-a-time in rehab, she came home, and what a day that was! How I loved having her at home. I loved being with my sweet pea. I loved waiting on her, lying next to her, eating with her, watching television together. Life was good.

Routine checkups found her clear of the cancer, and any fatal prognosis was avoided. Then, came May 9, 2015, just another routine checkup, after a mandated CAT-scan. When the doctor entered the room I knew things were not good. I could feel the cloud descend, the air being sucked out of the room. He told us Jackie had stage IV liver cancer, and there was an X-ray that I did not fathom to prove it.

"How could this be? The last check up revealed only healthy tissue. She was asymptomatic. This can't be true." I sat in silence—taking in the words. Then someone asked, "What do we do now?" That was the question. How do we beat this? How do I hang on to my Jackie? We all knew, including Jackie we weren't going to beat it, not this time. The handwriting was on the wall, and her days were numbered.

"Yes, she can undergo therapy, but at best, therapy will extend her life by maybe two months with no guarantee," the doctor said. "Moreover, the side effects of the chemotherapy could be painful, destroying any quality of life," he added.

"How long does she have to live?" I asked.

"With chemo. . . . maybe eight months. Without it . . . probably six." There it was. Like it or not. Her death sentence.

In our 80s, we know death awaited us, but we didn't dwell on the thought. But on this day, the sky turned dark, I could not swallow the lump in my throat, and figuratively speaking my world crashed. We left the office and ate lunch at a nearby restaurant, but I remember little if anything that was said.

Jackie seemed to be taking this news in stride, but I know she was dazed, numb, floored. The unavoidable truth was that my lady who saw herself as living forever wasn't going to make it. The doctor urged us to call hospice.

Hospice? Why hospice, I thought. She is asymptomatic. She is not sick, let alone dying. Denial is real; and on that day, the magnitude of the loss both of us were facing was too much for either of us to take in.

Again the decision whether or not to undergo chemotherapy was a decision Jackie had to make. After all, it was her life, not mine. This time I did not push her, and in her own good time, she chose to forgo any treatment. Hospice was called and thus began a relationship with some of the finest nurses and dearest individuals I have ever had the opportunity of knowing.

Hospice came twice a week. Laura was our nurse, and we soon loved her. Jackie looked forward to her coming. She became the keeper of the pills, and I or other family members were the dispensers of such medicine. Andrea, a social worker from hospice, spent time with me and let me cry on her shoulder.

The doctor encouraged us to get our house in order, to travel now if we so desired while Jackie was still able to experience quality living. So we packed the car for what we knew would be our last trip together. We tried not to think that way, but we knew the truth. Oregon, where our daughter, Diana, lived with her husband, Shawn, was our port of destination.

I love to drive, and nothing satisfied me more than having Jackie next to me as the miles flew by. The car provides privacy and the chance for just the two of us to be together in the same space experiencing the same moments, talking, sharing a good audio book, spontaneously reaching out and rubbing the other's thigh or holding each other's hand.

Life is in the journey, not in the destination. It took me years to finally understand that. When I was a child, my father would caution us before we took a trip: "Go to the bathroom because we are only going to stop for gas." As a little boy, I wouldn't have the urge, so I would climb into the back seat, and my dad would put his foot on the accelerator and down the highway we would fly. Inevitably, about an hour later, I would feel the urge and after trying unsuccessfully to deny that urge, I would tap my mother on the shoulder and tell her the nature beckoned and things were close to getting out of hand unless we stopped. My mother would intervene on my behalf and reluctantly my father would stop, reminding me that had I listened to him earlier, I would not be putting the family through this inconvenience. There was some great virtue put on bladder control in my family.

One thing was for sure: Life wasn't in the journey. There was no time to smell the roses; destination was everything. I, for one, find myself chuckling every time I see the bumper sticker "Are we having fun yet?" Because in my family the fun was frequently associated with the arrival—not the journey. Journey was to be endured to get to the fun of arrival.

Then I met Jackie and my days of driving straight through to Ohio non-stop, quickly greeting family and dropping in a heap to sleep for ten hours were over. Jackie saw life as a journey, not destination. On one occasion Jackie invited me to go with her to a workshop to be held in Albuquerque, on the condition that she got to call all the shots. I agreed and to my initial dismay and later pleasure, it took two days to go to Albuquerque. We stopped for coffee outside of Littleton, ate supper in Pueblo, spent the night in Walsenburg, ate breakfast the next day in Taos and then lunch in Santa Fe. The drive time should be eight hours, but we made it in two days; and I will never forget the delight of that trip because I saw so powerfully that it isn't *what* one does that matters; *who* one does it with is most important.

There we were, the two of us, for the last time journeying together. Time was moving too quickly, both of us in our own way celebrating and grieving at the same time. Our time in Oregon could not have been scripted better, including a limousine ride from Corvallis to Portland, a trip to the Rose Garden, a night in a luxury downtown hotel and a drive along the Oregon coast. The trip ended too soon, and then we were back in our beloved condo in Denver.

The weeks both flew by and dragged on. A death-watch is a hard thing to endure. Inch by inch, day by day, my lady wasted away. She fought to squeeze love and beauty out of every moment of consciousness. She welcomed children and grandchildren and invited them to talk and share their lives. She talked little about herself and only on several occasions about her impending death. The days stretched into weeks and then months, with comings and goings, and then Thanksgiving.

It was the last time she was able to gather at table with the family. The night before, she wanted to go to

Poppies for dinner. With great expenditure of effort she, with daughters Jodi and Diana at her side, made her way into the restaurant. She was mostly silent, shared a plate with me, barely ate and was so exhausted. I retrieved the wheelchair from the trunk of the car, and we made our way to the car and then home to sleep. At the Thanksgiving table the next day she picked at her food, struggled to understand the conversation, occasionally spoke and sometimes lost her thought mid-sentence.

The days ticked by with the awareness that the grim reaper was just outside the door. She struggled for each breath. At times I was sure she was gone, and then came another breath. She was a fighter. In her final days, she was unconscious, kept in that state of nothingness with the mercy of morphine. In one of her few lucid moments she said, "I love you."

In life and in death, she remained the most loving person I know. How I miss her. There is a hole in my soul wider than the Grand Canyon. At times I find myself keening, groaning; even now as I write tears silently stream down my face.

Jackie's death was not a tragedy. A tragedy is when a child or young person dies such as when our two sons died (my oldest son, John, drowned a few years ago.) The death of an 88-year-old woman, or in my case an 85-year-old man, is not a tragedy: such is the order of life; yet, for me, Jackie's passing continues to be a profound, unspeakable loss. I live feeling empty. My hope is in the Lord, and my faith is that I shall one day be with my Jackie again. I take comfort from the shorter catechism of the Presbyterian Church USA: "In life and in death, we belong to God." We belong not to each other but to God.

We loved to touch, loved to hold hands. Now, as I crawl in bed, there is no hand to hold, no arm to touch, no forehead to rub. There are only two pictures, one on each side of the bed to look at and to remember.

Everywhere I look in this home I see her palm prints. They are on the walls in the pictures that grace the living room. They are in the utensils that hang over the counter in the kitchen. They are on the bathroom mirror where sometimes I see not my face but hers. They are there in the ticking of the clock, the placement of the furniture, the polished table in the dining room, the rug on the floor in the living room. Her presence is felt everywhere, and I am thankful. No man could be so blessed.

I hold no regrets about our lives together. Of course we had ups and downs, but we enjoyed way more ups then downs. Of course there were moments of anger, but they never lasted long. Of course we experienced disappointment with the other, but that was rare. We were two fragmented people that found each other in brokenness and lived life together beyond our wildest imaginations. I smile thinking that for Jackie maybe I was just a problem to be solved. She always responded to the unexpected, no matter what the problem, with the words: "It is just a problem to be solved." Thanks for solving me, baby.

Early in our relationship, before we were married, as a beautiful evening together was ending, Jackie looked at me and said, "Les, be good to yourself. Treat yourself kindly." As I drove the twenty miles to the mountain cabin where I was living at the time I found myself unable to control the tears that splashed down my cheeks. No one ever said that to me. Here was a woman who affirmed me and believed that I was a person of worth. Most parting comments are admonitions: "Take care. Drive carefully. Watch out for other drivers or animals." Jackie's blessing stood far above any such comments. Just "be good to yourself, treat yourself kindly."

Jackie was not raised in the church and was not into formal religion. She never talked the God talk; she never felt guilty about not going to church, reading (or not reading) her Bible. She did not pray out loud. Though sometimes she read her Bible and prayed more than I did. She did not wear her religion on her sleeve, but I discovered she was more Christian than 99 percent of the professing Christians I knew as a minister. She wrestled with the big questions as do I. Questions about the meaning of life, God, the hereafter. I suspect most thinking people do.

After that night when she so affirmed me I knew she was something special, and I would be so blessed if she would agree to spend her life with me. That she did, and the blessings abounded and, yes, still abound. I am a better, more together, whole person for having her in my life.

Maya Angelou said,

"I've learned that people will forget what you said, people will forget what you did, but people will never forget how you made them feel."

Often, I think about what Jackie said, and I certainly remember what she did; but most of all I remember how she made me (and others) feel. She called forth the best in me.

Chapter 9

My Thoughts about Truth

One Sunday afternoon, I found myself channel surfing and stumbled onto Channel 41. I had never watched Channel 41, a religious station in Denver, but I became drawn in by a woman interviewing a guest. "I know that woman," I said to myself. "Why, that is —."

Like so many religious shows, always there is the sense of everything is perfect with Jesus. All one needs do is just trust and all things will be wonderful. The message is that deliverance is always there for the asking. I suspect such comes from our desire to go back to the Garden of Eden, that place of perfection from which we have been banished. But I recognized the woman whose television ministry was now flashing before me, and I knew her to be a deeply-troubled individual because I had been her pastor. I knew her life wasn't as wonderful as she professed. The truth is that in this world, every day with Jesus is not necessarily sweeter than the day before. The truth is that deliverance doesn't always happen.

The program that followed featured Jimmy Swaggart. I hadn't seen Jimmy on television since the revelation of his encounters with prostitutes on Airline Highway in Atlanta that rocked the nation. I wondered if his fall from grace had humanized him; so I watched. Before, when he was at the top of his game, he always came across to me as angry, now he came across as beaten down. He aged badly. I suspect going through what he did would give anyone gray hairs. Then, he made a remark that went like this: "There are those of you watching who can show me no grace, and if you can't show me grace then God can't show grace to you." Apart from his statement being defensive, it struck me as pretty poor theology.

Grace and acceptance doesn't mean carte blanche approval. Acceptance and approval are two words with different meanings, yet many are unable to see the difference. My children did all kinds of things I do not approve of, but there has never been a time I did not accept them. I cannot conceive of disowning them or not loving them. And gratefully, I experience acceptance from them. There have been all kinds of things I have done my children did not approve of, but I know I was accepted and loved, at least I need to believe that. We can live without approval, although approval is nice to receive; but we cannot live for very long without acceptance.

140

Acceptance means living in the world as *it is*, not as we think life *ought to be*. Frequently, this means living with pain, settling for less than the ideal. I suspect that more Christians than we like to acknowledge live with pain. They suffer as I did and do with their children. I know I am not alone. They know they were not all they could have been or should have been as parents. No one ever does that job perfectly.

I long, if not literally, certainly emotionally, to be near my children. I want them to understand how much I love them. I don't long to change them. They enjoy a right to live their lives as they so desire. I believe we don't need our parents to agree with us, especially if we feel loved and heard. God knows my boys gave me a run for my money, but then they can say the same for me. All in all ours has been a great adventure.

Truth: Lowercase truth/Uppercase TRUTH

I feel like a man without a country regarding doctrine. I don't know where I land in the evangelical church. I know I do not spout the party line of most who call themselves evangelical. I am aware that many who classify themselves as evangelicals will not number me in their camp. Here is the catch. For all of my doubts and uncertainties I believe in the atonement, that Jesus came and died for the sins of the world and that he rose from the dead. What am I missing here? Isn't that what evangelicals believe?

I guess my departure from evangelicals is that I no longer am as certain about TRUTH as I once was, and certainty is desired among so many true believers. Uppercase TRUTH has to do with that which can be scientifically proven as well as experiences that defy explanation such as love, courage, integrity. My love for

141

Jackie is uppercase TRUTH which comes from my experience with her. Love transcends description. If you have not experienced it you cannot know that it is uppercase TRUTH, as true as any scientific fact.

Lowercase truth tells you what I believe about something, be it religion, politics or simply my view of life. What must be remembered is that just because I believe something my belief does not make it true. The difficulty is that often lowercase truth is seen as uppercase TRUTH. When that happens, certainty cuts off dialogue with others who hold a different view about religion, politics, life. How easy it is for assumptions to become certainty. Certainty just may be the enemy of understanding.

In my fundamentalist days, certainty ruled. I had the answer for almost everything, and since I had the TRUTH there was no need for discussion. Now I see how often I mistook lowercase truth for uppercase TRUTH. Just maybe mistaking lowercase truth for uppercase TRUTH is why we see thousands of different denominations, all of which claim that their view is the TRUE view, the right view.

Growing up I was told a good way to witness is to ask a person, "If you died tonight do you know you will go to Heaven? If the person said they were not sure, I was to tell them they could be sure then invite them to say the sinner's prayer, which was to guarantee certainty.

Now I believe in Heaven, and I believe when I die I will go there, but I must live through the experience of death to know. Just because I believe something doesn't make it true. In a short time I will go to the store for groceries and then return. I believe with all my heart that I will do that safely: that I will arrive at the store safely and will return safely. After all, I made that trip hundreds of times, but even with that awareness I must live the experience of my trip to the store and back to know for certain. Many folks believed they were going to go somewhere only to experience a mishap and not get there.

Moreover, isn't the Christian life supposed to be a life of faith—not a life of certainty? Isn't faith defined as the substance of things hoped for, the evidence of things not seen (Hebrews 11:1)? Things hoped for. Hope is a wonderful thing, and my hope is in Heaven. Things hoped for the evidence not seen. I want to believe in certainty that the evidence is seen. Still the Bible declares: "The just shall live by faith" (Romans 1:17), The declaration is not that the just shall live by certainty, but by faith.

What I want is certainty, but the Christian walk does not promise that.

When I think of it I am confronted with the TRUTH that faith is something that is not optional, it is mandated because the Bible declares, and experience has taught me, that "No one knows what the future holds" (Ecclesiastes 8:7). I do not know what the next moment, hour, day, month, year holds. I must live it to know, and I believe that is the way God intends it to be.

At times I find myself troubled by those with serious doubts about religion, but I am far more troubled by those with terrible certainties. Such people cannot enter into dialogue, for they already know with certainty the answers to life's troubling questions.

Heresy of Certainty

The heresy of certainty is at the heart of all cults. Cult members are by definition closed off to seriously considering another viewpoint, and why should they? For they already have the TRUTH, uppercase truth. To allow the consideration of alternate views would mean risking the unraveling of their world of certainty. I hold my beliefs, that which I believe to be true, and when it comes to the future most of them are lowercase truth. Thus, I believe that one mark of maturity is the ability to tolerate ambiguity. Always there are questions, that which I do not understand.

The truth that there is much I do not understand does not mean that I do not have convictions or causes, or that I refuse to work for change. Still, ultimately, I am faced with another truth and that is that I can change myself, but I cannot change others. There is the freedom that can come in just trusting the process, going with the flow, giving up on trying to hold back the river, being available to what is, staying in tune, not resisting. There is a sense, as paradoxical as it may seem, that doing such things just may be the ultimate in taking control. There is a humility in submitting, for in doing so, I confess that most often I do not know with certainty just how everything will work out.

I am really talking about the balance in working for change and accepting what is, in struggling and in relinquishing or letting go. The inner journey calls us to let go, submit, relinquish, trust. The outer journey calls us to resist, hang on, and insist on change. And always there is that never-ending tension. There is the understanding that I am only a person who is limited, fallible, incomplete and also the highest of God's creation with unlimited potential, and I can effect change. I am also a person who seeks to understand the difference between TRUTH (uppercase) and truth (lowercase).

Chapter 10

Words that Changed My Life

Do words really make a difference?

My hope soared for Thomas when we had good talks. But talk doesn't change people. Jackie asked me one day how many times in my life I changed because of what someone said. The question staggered me, because as a minister who trades in words and wants to believe that all those sermons I preached made up of words has made a difference in people's lives, I had trouble thinking of any times I changed because of what someone said to me. A few days later, I was able to identify three times when my life changed because of words.

I recall my mother's words of comfort at the revival the summer I was nine. After a hellfire and brimstone message at a revival meeting at First Baptist, my mother said something like this, "You are not going to hell. Jesus loves you and so do I." Those words changed my life. I am not sure how, but I know her being there that night with me was life-changing. I don't know when Jesus and I got it on, but I know we did, and my relationship with Him changed my life. I more and more agree with Thomas when he wrote he was being saved daily and continually.

The second time words changed my life was when I believed I was unworthy to be a minister, consumed by guilt of conceiving my son before marriage. (See "Month Counters" in Chapter 1.) That day in the seminary when Dr. Grounds put his arm around me and said, "As an agent of Jesus Christ, I want you to hear that God forgives you. And as the dean of this seminary, I want you to hear that I don't want you to leave school." Up until that time I saw God as a judgmental god—out to get those who did bad things.

That day, through the words spoken to me by Dr. Grounds, was the first time I was consciously aware of the love of God breaking on my life. My life changed because of what a man said. He told me he wanted me to stay in school, and I did, and that changed my life because those words changed my view of God. I stopped seeing Him as out to get me and started experiencing Him as loving me like I had never been loved before. Grace overflowed.

The third time words changed my life describes how after leaving the church, I got loved right back into the church.

While in my final quarter of training to become a supervisor of Clinical Pastoral Education, I received an unexpected call. It was from Howard Childers, the minister at St. James Presbyterian Church. I knew Howard as we were in a small group together. He knew I was in CPE training, much of which involved training to be a counselor. Now he asked me if I might be open to coming to St. James to serve part-time as a counselor. He told me that St. James was composed of a lot of hurting people and he did not have time to respond to all the demands.

I really held no desire to get involved in another church, but I was keenly aware that I could not become a supervisor of Clinical Pastoral Education without being endorsed by a denomination. I was aware that such an endorsement would not come from the Baptist denomination I was involved with prior to my divorce. Perhaps if I counseled at St. James the Presbytery of Denver could somehow endorse me.

So I became a part-time counselor at St. James. I did not desire to attend the services at St. James, but needing exposure as the newest member of the staff, I knew I needed to show up.

I was totally unprepared for what happened when I started attending the services of the church. I never heard a preacher like Howard. He shared his life, his struggles, his victories and defeats from the pulpit. I found myself absorbed by his honesty, his realness. He refused to play the role of the put-together pastor who because of his walk with Jesus was above the struggles of common folk. It became apparent that his vulnerability attracted so many hurting people. In fact Howard referred to St. James as, "The church for losers."

I knew I felt like a loser. I would sit through Sunday morning services embarrassed as I was unable to stop the tears from silently sliding down my cheeks. If I could share my life like he shared his, just maybe I could go back and pastor a church. But where, I asked myself would I ever find another church like St. James?

Howard did go to bat for me with the Denver Presbytery, and because of his efforts I was accepted into membership of the Presbytery as an assistant pastor at St. James Presbyterian Church. My problem of finding a denomination, which would endorse me as a supervisor of Clinical Pastoral Education, was now solved.

One Sunday morning, Howard stood up to preach and shocked those of us in the congregation.

"I have my sermon but I am not going to preach it today; and unless any of you have something to say, I am going to suggest that we sing a song, have the benediction and go home." I could not believe what I was hearing. I thought, *so you may have had something painful happen in your life. Now suck it up and deliver. The show must go on!*

As I sat there in shock, you could have heard a pin drop as others in the congregation sat in stunned silence. Then a voice was heard from the congregation, "I have something to say."

"Come up here and say it," Howard responded. Slowly one of the leaders of the church made his way to the pulpit.

"Howard," he said. "When my dad died you came over to the house. I don't remember anything you said, but I do remember that you sat with me throughout that afternoon with your arm around my shoulder. I can't tell you how much that meant to me. I never thanked you for being there for me, and so now I am thanking you." With that he stepped down and returned to his seat.

Now another stood saying he also had something to say. And so it went on that never-to-be-forgotten Sunday. One member of the congregation after another stood and encouraged their pastor. It was the parishioners pastoring their pastor as time stood still; and there was not a dry eye in the house as all who were there witnessed something beautiful on that October morning.

Then, a few weeks later, Howard up and resigned. I felt betrayed. How could he! How dare he! Why would he leave? I saw him as my protector, my mentor, one who was teaching me so much about what it was to really minister. Now he was leaving, and the light went out in my heart.

To my surprise, a few weeks after Howard left, the session asked me to attend one of their meetings. I knew what they wanted. I knew they wanted my resignation, and by George, they could have it! Now that Howard was gone I felt utterly vulnerable — a man questioning most everything, one in the middle of a faith crisis.

I entered the meeting with a huge chip on my shoulder. The session moderator welcomed me and then said, "We called you here tonight because we are looking for an Interim pastor while we seek a full-time minister. We would like you to be that Interim pastor."

Stunned I said, "How could you want me as your pastor, don't you know I am in the middle of a divorce?"

"Yes, we are aware of that, and it must be very painful for you and for Ann. We pray for the two of you, but right now we need a pastor. You are a pastor, aren't you?"

Truth be told, I didn't know what I was or what I believed, but I became their pastor while they looked for a pastor and later I became the pastor they were looking for and remained with that church for losers, of whom I was the biggest, for the next 22 years. During those 22 years, I started winning more than I was losing.

The words that changed my life were: "Would you be our pastor while we look for a pastor?"

Do words really make a difference? Can they change a life? As I pondered Jackie's question, I became aware that in each situation it wasn't *what* was said but *what followed* that mattered. When I was nine, when an evangelist had no time for a small boy, a mother's love for her son made the difference. A mother's love has no end. In the second case at seminary, a dean lived out the forgiveness he offered that day with acceptance and caring. I am thankful for that man whom I continued to meet with for decades until his death and whose life continued to grace mine with love and acceptance. In the third case, a church modeled acceptance and love in ways I'd never seen before. This church cheered me on and called forth the best in me, loving me into a sense of wholeness. I was blessed to serve in their midst.

The common denominator in each of the three circumstances was love.

Why The Question

And why had Jackie asked that question of me? "Les, how many times in your life has anyone said anything that actually changed your life?" Because she knew that I still wanted to believe that I could talk my gay son Thomas into change, and she knew that wasn't going to work.

"If talk would do it, Thomas would have changed a long time ago," she said. And then she added, "We can love him. If anything will work, it won't be talk. It will be love. And if someday, he does kill himself, and he may, we will know we gave him as much love as we had to give. If we err, let's err on the side of grace and love."

It's not that words aren't important. I am sure others have said significant things that changed my life. As a kid, I used to say, "Sticks and stones may break my bones, but words will never hurt me." Of course, that isn't true. One thing I learned is that although words may not break your bones, they can break your heart. Words possess the power to heal and destroy; and if this is so, they also hold the power to heal and to bring life.

Now in this country, gay marriages are legal whether one likes it or not. Since such marriages are legal, why should the church not accept gay married people asking of them what supposedly the church asks of hetero-sexual marriages, namely faithfulness, fidelity to one partner unless the union is broken by death or divorce?

It would be naive to think that the problem of infi-delity among Christian married homosexuals would only be limited to non-Christian homosexuals. Who is not aware that infidelity among Christian heterosexuals is not limited to non-Christians? The same would be true of homosexual Christians. I am arguing for an even playing field in the church rather than *don't ask, don't tell.*

I am aware now that most couples — both Christians and non-Christians — who date for six weeks are sexu-ally active, and yet, the church continues to sound the call to celibacy. Celibacy is set forth as biblical ideal, even though most ministers are aware that in the vast majority of heterosexual Christian weddings involve a couple living together or at least sleeping together. Living together for Christians and non-Christians is common in our time. The avalanche of Christian hetero-sexuals who engage in sex before marriage has over-whelmed the church, which for the most part has not and will not address the issue. The church, like society, chooses to ignore the matter perhaps because there seems no effective strategy to change the situation; and maybe that is all right. My hope would be that the church would stop this inordinate focus on sex between two monogamous individuals.

I conclude that what goes on between two consenting adults—whether heterosexual or homosexual—who love one another is not the business of the church. Our business is the business of love. Let's let God do the judging.

this is the church going along w/ society vs. standing its ground + pushing back

Chapter 11

Grief Endured

On an unseasonably warm January day we gathered at the Memorial Garden at St. James Church to spread Jackie's ashes. I slip my hand into the urn and sprinkle a handful of whitish ash on a rose plant in the rose garden there, sacred ground. The ash falls on the remains of our oldest son whose urn was buried there four years ago. I dip again and sprinkle around the roots of what certainly appears to be a dead rose bush, but who faith tells me will bloom in the spring. At a later date some of Thomas' ashes will be spread here.

Jackie's ashes feel like powdered sugar and I find the fingers of my right hand, now white with her ashes brushing against my lips. I murmur, "I want to taste you just one more time."

Almost ten years ago I wrote her a love letter.

To my Jackie-

You are the wind beneath my sails. You cheer me on when I feel discouraged, lift me up when I feel depressed. Your smile warms my soul, pointing me to move toward the positive. The soft and soothing lilt of your voice soothes and quiets me. I love your voice. Each morning is beautiful because you are here.

Wasn't it only yesterday that we met and married? Where have the years gone? Almost 33 of them have sped by. The days since knowing you have been the best days of my life. Our days have been filled with sunshine because of the person you are.

We struggled together, mostly with children, rather than ourselves. In our struggles you kept on loving me through the good and the bad. You have been to my children grace incarnate, loving them as if they had been yours by birth. You have the rare gift of seeing and bringing out the good in others.

You care for and nurture me always calling forth the best in me. You bless and do not curse, even when I give you reasons for doing so. At times when you question the wisdom of my choices, you still support me in them.

Our travels throughout this country and the world draw us closer to each other. Traveling is our excuse for carving out unencumbered time with each other. Traveling is about us more than places to go or things to see. It is being together and having each other exclusively for ourselves. Particularly is that true when we take automobile trips. Ahead is the road, a good book, our touch, our attention on each other with nothing to distract us. I love being with you day in and day out, but especially I love traveling with you.

You have a God-given beautiful sense of timing. Often you know what I am thinking and amaze me by verbalizing my thoughts. Sometimes when needed, in a soft caring way you correct me, ever so gently turn me, and move me from disaster. You never put me down. Even when I put myself down, you build me up. You have given to me your body and soul and in turn I seek to do the same.

Our love is rare, a thing of beauty. You are so precious to me. Many folks only recognize how fortunate they are to have each other after one is gone. I have known it since the day you agreed to live out your life with me.

I love your taste in decorating, the love that comes through to me in the food you prepare. Your goodness and kindness has transformed me into a far better person then I would have ever been had God not allowed our lives to entangle. I love you, I love you, I love you. Thank you for loving me.

Chapter 12

The Challenge of Diminishment

Growing Old

Every stage of life has its challenges. There are the challenges of childhood, of teenage years, of adulthood, but I think the challenge of growing old is the most challenging because the future is so quickly shrinking. At every other stage there is that which seemingly stretches somewhat endlessly before you. In other stages there is always a belief of a future in this world. Now I know the sand in the hourglass of time for me in this world is rapidly running out. In that awareness, the old, looking-forward-to kinds of things no longer buffer me from the reality of death.

Diminishment is what now marks life, losses, and limitations. The phone rings and I am told that I "just won a free Caribbean cruise." Whereas 15 years ago, I would have jumped for joy. Now I hang up before the recorded voice can tell me where to sign up.

The things that once filled my life (travel, work, gardening, cycling, the list goes on), no longer give me the satisfaction they once did. Because of diminishment I can no longer do as much as I once did, but also even if I can there is less interest in doing so.

Back in 2003, I wrote the following article:

> *I just turned 72, but I do not feel "old." I do not like to think about "old." My propensity is to do what most of my peers do, namely deny old. Maybe if we just don't talk about it, think about it, old will somehow mysteriously go away.*
>
> *Yet even a moment's reflection leaves me at 72 with the awareness that if I should live for another 10 or 15 years, and I hope I do, I will be old. Ten or 15 years is a relatively short time in the life span of a 72-year-old person. When one steps over that invisible line of elderly to old varies; but sooner or later, unless I die on the way to old, it will happen.*
>
> *In thinking about old I found myself naming people in their late 70s and 80s who I look forward to being with. Ironically, my list was short, topping out at six. Six names were all that came to mind of old people in whose presence I delight. I was taken back for I expected the list to be far more extensive. Over the years as a pastor, I have known hundreds of old people. I've visited them in their homes and in*

nursing homes, but I confess that often such visits were obligatory and as short as possible.

I found myself asking why my list of those I love to spend time with is so short and then it struck me that the folks on my short list all share an amazing number of common characteristics that mark them as beautiful people.

For example, without exception they are kind, gracious, and loving. They are individuals who always affirm others. They are grateful and thankful for the gifts life has given them and in tune with the joy of the present moment. I was aware that my elderly friends are intellectually stimulating, eclectic, remaining open to new ideas and new experiences. Each is as active as they can be within the confines of what it means to be old. They are non-critical, refusing to be locked into just one way of viewing life.

It dawned on me that every one of the six is informed. They read widely and are comfortable with those who are younger than they are. They enjoy numerous younger friends, refusing to confine themselves to people who are only of their generation.

Oh yes, the people on my short list are also good listeners, able to skillfully move the focus from themselves to the other. One has to work hard to get them to tell their own stories; they much prefer to listen to mine. They display minimal ego needs, are highly flexible, and able to accept what life requires of them.

My older friends rarely talk about their aches and pains. Although they experience them, despite the indignities of old age and physical infirmity, they choose not to dwell on such things.

Finally, without exception they are servants. When I am in their presence, my elderly friends are always concerned about my comfort.

My older friends are lovers of peace. They seek to avoid confrontational conflict in personal relationships. Each has a non-critical, positive attitude, in-spite of tough times.

A minister friend of mine told me of an old man, a rather famous former pastor, who so richly blessed his life. He told me that if his phone rang at 9:00 p.m. on a Saturday night he knew who would be on the line. His old friend would say something like this, "What are you preaching on tomorrow?" My friend would tell him and then the old pastor would inevitably say, "That sounds just great. I wish I could be there. Let's take a minute to pray that God will use your sermon to touch lives." Then he would pray and hang up.

My friend told me that not once did that dear old man every say, "You know I preached on that passage at least a half dozen times during my ministry, let me tell you what I said." "All he did," my friend said, "was affirm me." What a gift from an old minister to a younger one, the gift of affirmation.

I want to be like that when in my not-too-distant future I become "old." What is sobering is the awareness that if such is to happen it will not be by accident. It will be intentional. As I thought about my old friends, I became aware that they are not that much different in their old age than they were in their 40s and 50s. They each spent the better part of a lifetime becoming what they are. They worked at it. They chose to see the glass half full rather than half empty. They chose to be flexible and resisted the temptation to rigidity. They understand that we either bend or break, change or die. It seems to be true both emotionally and physically. My friends choose, and keep on choosing, to bend rather than break, to change rather than die. They do so understand that the day will

come when unable to any longer bend they will break,
and unable to any longer change they will die. They
are at peace with that reality. Such choices are not
easy and maybe that is why their number is so few. It
is not easy to grow old graciously.

What my short list of old friends call forth in me
is my better self. They say to me without knowing
"this is what you can hope to become." Maybe at 72
it is not yet too late.

So now at 85 the question comes often: Les how
are you doing at being old? My answer is pretty much,
"I guess it depends on who you ask?" What has overwhelmed me at 85 is the extent of the losses I face. I
am referring to the seemingly never-ending loss of
dear friends and loved ones. These days my face is
continually being pushed into the mud of mortality.
On Saturday I will attend yet another funeral and on
Tuesday fly to Moab, Utah to spend three days with an
old friend whose wife just died. From diagnosis to her
death was just 13 days, and as you can imagine his life
is upside down.

I am aware with the loss of Jackie that there is an
emptiness inside that I never dreamed at 72 could be so
hollow. I am also aware that at 85 there is not enough
time left to ever seek another relationship and there
is certainly no other woman like Jackie. There is the
desire to be sure for another deep, meaningful relationship with another woman, but there is, as I see it, not
enough time.

The challenge of being alone is mixed with loneliness and often emptiness. Missed most is not having
anyone to process life with on an ongoing basis. This is
what I miss: the simple sitting day in and day out with
another to share a cup of coffee and talk about the day, a

hand to hold before falling asleep at night, lips to touch as I depart, eyes to look deeply into and once again mouth "I love you."

I once asked Jackie when we go from "getting old" to "old" and her answer was "you can step across the line anytime you like, but know this. I will always just be "getting old." And so at nearly 89, when she died she was never "old", just "getting old." And not being "old" but just "getting old" served her well. Internally, she never aged and never lost her lust for life.

A friend of mine once said that which I do not forget. "Life doesn't shout; it just runs out." So day by day as life winds down I confess in the midst of the awareness of losses that I am the most blessed of men. I am grateful for each new day, more aware of colors, of fresh air, of the beauty of creation around me, aware of my joy in watching little children at play.

Chapter 13

The Deaths of Two Friends

Ray's Message

It was Mark Twain who said; "It ain't what you don't know that gets you in trouble, it's what you do know for sure the just ain't so."

What I knew for sure since earliest memories and right up until the confusion of the latter years of my first marriage was that I had the truth. End of discussion. There was no place for doubt, ambiguity or mystery, no place for entertaining other views. I did not associate let alone open myself up to other perspectives. "Come out from them and be ye separate and touch not the unclean thing" (II Corinthians 6:17) When at Fort Logan I found myself in the midst of what I always thought were unclean people and unclean things, folks I never associated with on anything but a superficial level prior to my Clinical Pastoral Education (CPE); yet, what I experienced was that they genuinely accepted and, yes, loved me.

Let me be clear here. I have dear Christian friends who graced my life and who I love dearly who do not agree with me. I hope I am not their project to change, and I have no interest in seeking to change them. They often see what I call lowercase truth as uppercase TRUTH. Just maybe they are right. Only in God's timing will any of us know.

I love 1 Corinthians 13:12-13: "For now we see in a mirror dimly, but then we shall see face to face. Now I know only in part, then (at some future time) I will know fully, even as I am fully known. And now faith, hope and love abide and the greatest of these is love."

After my divorce there were dear friends who disappeared from my life. For whatever reason they were not around. One was my old homiletics professor at Denver Seminary. Throughout my school experience, he was like a father to me. After graduation, for the next 13 years, I met with him weekly for his counsel and wisdom. No appointment was needed, I stopped by his office, and he dropped what he was doing and off we went to the nearest coffee shop. As years passed, I felt free to address him by his first name, Ray.

During and after my divorce I missed my weekly sessions with Ray. Once I stopped by his office and he was not in, I left him a note expressing my desire to get together, to hear from him, but he did not respond.

The years rolled by, and then one day I heard he was suffering from cancer, not expected to live for more than a few months. That day uninvited I went to the hospital, and walked into his room. He was surprised to see me, taken back when I said, "I don't know if you want to see me, but I want to see you. I intend to visit you at least twice a week whether you want me to or not, for the truth is I love you. I won't stay long but whether you like it or not I am coming." And so I went twice a week. Once when I arrived and asked him how he was doing, he said to me, "I'm tired. I have had too many visitors today." I said, "I don't care how many visitors you have had, I am still coming. I won't stay long, but I will come."

When he was discharged from the hospital I took him out for dinner. Once a large man, now he was but a shadow of his former self, and he needed to lean on me as we entered the restaurant. As I ate and he picked at his food, I asked him, "If you were given another year to live what would you like to do? He spoke of wanting to finish a book he was writing on preaching, of wanting to spend more time with his wife and his children. Then we hit the silent years, all those years when he and I were separated. He said, "I wanted to write, I wanted to call, but I didn't know what to write or what to say, so I did neither." I responded, "It doesn't matter. All that matters is that we are back together now."

Then the day came when I was told he only had hours to live. I immediately went to the hospital. The family was gathered around his bed, and I joined them. Ray motioned for me to come closer and said, "Now for the great mystery." I knew he was thinking of 1 Corinthians 15:51, "Listen I will tell you a mystery! We will not all die, but we will all be changed." Then Paul goes on to proclaim the hope of the resurrection.

As I left Ray's room, knowing I will never see him alive again, I heard him calling my name. I turned and his hand was raised in a weak wave and he spoke: "Les, I will see you again, in due time." Indeed I believe he will.

Seeking to Love the Best Way I Know How

So there is much I don't know, much that is a mystery, but this I do know: that my God is a God of love (I John 4:8). And I know that when Jesus encounters a lawyer who asks him "Teacher, which commandment in the law is the greatest?" Jesus responds, "You shall love the Lord your God with all your heart, and with all your soul, and with all your mind. This is the greatest and first commandment. And a second is like it: You shall love your neighbor as yourself." I understand Jesus' words to mean as I love my neighbor I also love God. Jesus issues my call to love in John 13:35 where he says, "By this everyone will know that you are my disciples, if you have love for one another."

"The unexamined life is not worth living," so says Socrates. Many would suggest that I spend too much time examining, too much time navel gazing. Be that as it may, that is the way I am wired.

So there are things I now believe that at one time I did not believe, but so many of them are lowercase truth—most of them having to do with the future. Whereas once I saw lowercase truth as uppercase TRUTH, now I am comfortable living with mystery, ambiguity, yes, even doubt. It wasn't always so, but because of my lady Jackie's impact on my life and my son Thomas' teaching me so much it has become so.

I am less obsessed with being right, less certain, more at peace with living out the questions, but at the same time more certain that in the midst of my questions, my uncertainties, that God loves me even when I don't feel it.

Soon my earthly journey will end. Meanwhile, I live each day being as fully alive as possible, grateful for what is given, not angry for what is taken away. I need the good and the bad, needed all that happened and yet will happen. It is because of where I have been that I am who I am. Through it all, in looking back, often undetected at the time, was God at work, invested in my life, saying without speaking, "Les, it isn't what happens to you that matters, what matters is what you are learning from what happens to you." My prayer continues to be: "God help me to be a lover and a learner."

My mother in the latter years of her life asked me why I questioned everything. "Why can't you just accept?" My answer was I don't know why. Part of me wishes I just could accept; life would be much simpler.

While taking a class in college called Junior Doctrine, a student asked the professor a question. I don't remember the question, but I have never forgotten the answer. The professor responded, "Who do you think you are, you young whippersnapper, to question Calvin, Luther, Zwingli, the great expositors of the faith? Listen to what I say, write it down, believe it, it is the truth." The putdown was chilling, and so I withdrew from questioning. Who am I, little old me, to doubt? Write it down. End of discussion. This was the truth once and for all delivered to the saints.

I have always been attracted to Dietrich Bonhoeffer. To me he was a saint, anything but what I am. Involving himself in a plot to assassinate Adolf Hitler, he was exposed and executed just prior to the end of World War

II. When I first read about him and his refusal to leave Germany even when he had the opportunity, I wrestled with the question of what I might have done had I been a minister in that country at that time. After all my mother's parents immigrated to the United States from Germany, and with German blood flowing through my veins it is not farfetched to ask the question about my own courage. I knew then and I know now that I probably would have taken the path of least resistance as did most of the clergy in Nazi Germany. Gratefully that test was not mine to take.

Then I came across a poem by Bonhoeffer written shortly before his death, and I found it both comforting and troubling. More than anything it was that which I could identify with, for this saint also struggled, wondered, doubted, experienced fear and a sense of abandonment, just like me.

Not all of what he wrote in that poem can I identify with for I was never in prison as he was; but the latter part I can identify with: the conflicting feelings, the paradox of believing and doubting. The poem is called "Who Am I," and the part I identify with most goes like this:

......Am I then really that which other men tell of?
Or am I only what I myself know of myself?
Restless and longing and sick, like a bird in a cage,
Struggling for breath, as though hands were
     compressing my throat,
Yearning for colors, for flowers, for the voice
     of birds,
Thirsting for words of kindness, for neighborliness,
Tossing in expectations of great events,
Powerlessly trembling for friends at an infinite
     distance.

Weary and empty at praying, at thinking,
*   at making,*
Faint and ready to say farewell to it all.

Who am I? This or the other?
Am I one person today and tomorrow another?
Am I both at once? A hypocrite before others.
And before myself a contemptible woebegone
*   weakling?*
Or is something within me still like a beaten army
Fleeing in disorder from victory already achieved?
*   Who am I? They mock me, these lonely*
*   questions of mine.*
Whoever I am, Thou knowest, O God, I am Thine"

So I wonder, question, doubt, and doubt my doubts. It's an unending wrestling with the angel like Jacob of old. Only even though Jacob would not let go until he received the blessing and his name was changed to Israel, so I wrestle, simply because I can do no other, even though I receive the blessing multiple times in my life and continue to have it. A blessing undeserved, all of grace granted to me by a God who is not troubled by my questioning, my doubts, fears, anxieties, a God who has met me and left me mostly comfortable with ambiguity, mystery and wonderings, and paradox.

Trudy's Message

During the years I was the minister at St. James Church, I officiated at numerous funerals, played the role of the professional. Now I set aside that role, and am just another 85-year-old man who asks questions. Some of the questions I ask are: How much of my life can I still control? After I am gone will I be missed?

Am I ready to die? When I am gone, will anyone know who I was or what I once did? If they know, will anyone care?

I am not aware of being depressed or enjoying life any less in asking such questions. I am simply aware of passages — of the relentless march of time, and with that awareness the treasuring of each day.

One Sunday after church, a man named John asked me if I would visit him and his wife. "Of course," I said. "When can I come over?"

"Well, it is not quite as simple as that, you see my wife Trudy is in the hospital, and she wants to speak with you. Can you come to Rose Hospital at seven o'clock on Tuesday evening?" I found it strange that John would be making a date for a hospital visit. In those days, pastors had access to patients in hospitals whenever they were able to stop by. This was my first encounter with John. I did not know him or his wife Trudy, for the St. James Church now numbered more than a thousand people, so it was impossible for me to know all who attended.

Agreeing to the terms of the visit, the following Tuesday at seven in the evening, I entered Trudy's room. John welcomed me as I came through the door. I was surprised to find Trudy sitting up in bed. She had taken pains to dress, and someone, if not she herself, had carefully applied make up and neatly combed her hair.

We barely exchanged greetings when she asked me, "Would you do my funeral?"

Taken aback, for the 40-year-old woman sitting before me looked anything but like she was about to die, I said, "How long do you have to live?"

"The doctor's tell me between seven and ten days. You see I have leukemia, and my body is no longer responding to the blood transfusions. There is nothing more that can be done."

"Of course I will do your funeral," I said.

After talking about her impending death, her pain in having to say goodbye to her two young children, I said, "Obviously you put a great deal of thought to this. What would you like me to say at your funeral?"

Without a moment's hesitation, she said, "You tell them that life is a gift. Never take it for granted. Live every day as fully as you can. Take time to be present to the things that matter, the people around you, beauty, little things. You tell them that life is a gift and never distain it, treasure every moment of it granted to you."

Ten days later I stood in front of the people at St. James Church telling them, "Life is a gift, never take it for granted. Live every day as fully as you can. Take time to be present to the things that matter, the people around you, beauty, little things. Treasure every moment given you."

Now in the twilight years of my life I often think of Trudy, even though she has been gone for years. At this stage of my life I more than ever know Trudy was right. Life is a gift; never take it for granted. Live every day to the fullest. There is a great deal that I have done in my life that I would like to undo, but none of us are offered a do-over option. Bottom line: when I look across the 85 years of my life I am aware of God's hand in so much of what has happened to me even when I didn't think God was anywhere to be found.

There are a lot of things I am less certain of now. I still know I am on the journey and that I seek to live every day to the fullest. It is true that I offer fewer answers than I once had. It is also true that I live with mystery, ambiguity, the unanswered question, and yes even my doubts; but one thing I am absolutely certain of is God's patience and love for me knows no bounds.

When preaching at St. James, I ended each Sunday service incorporating Jackie's blessing, the words she first blessed me with all those years ago when I stood on her doorstep and she said to me as I prepared to leave, "Les, be good to yourself, treat yourself kindly". Now, I end this book with the same blessing given to the people at St. James. It goes like this: "As you leave this place (close this book) know that almost everyone you meet carries a heavy load. If you scratch beneath the surface of most any life you will discover tremendous pain, it is there. So be good to yourself, and kind to your neighbor. Don't be afraid to put your arm around your own shoulder or that of a friend. Go in the love of Jesus and celebrate!"

About the Author

L es came to Denver in 1953 to attend seminary. After graduation, his ministerial career was spent at three different parishes in the Denver area, For 22 years, he ministered at St. James Presbyterian Church in Littleton, Colorado, retiring as senior minister. Since retirement, he has served as interim pastor at numerous Denver area churches. Les is a retired supervisor of Clinical Pastoral Education (CPE) as well as diplomat in the College of Pastoral Supervision and Psychotherapy (CPSP). Les is an avid bicyclist who has listened to hundreds of talking books while riding more than 150,000 miles since retiring. He is registered to compete at the National Senior Games in Birmingham AL in 2017, racing his bike in the 85 to 90 age division in the 5K and 10K time trials and 20K and 40K road races. He enjoyed 43 years of marriage to his late wife Jackie who passed away in 2015. Les has six children, 14 grand-children, and 10 great grandchildren.

Did Thomas have friends who
were not homosexual

p.100 - life is about the
journey, the destination
p.134 will take care of itself

p.105 son, Thomas, 4 themes in
his journals - 2 are:
love of homeless
love of Jesus
when he served the homeless
he served Jesus

published 2017
p.127 Words hold the power
to devastate

p.136 In life + in death
we belong to God.

p.141 top - acceptance

" TRUTH - experience
of seeing someone live
their faith

CPSIA information can be obtained
at www.ICGtesting.com
Printed in the USA
LVOW07s1926030817
543647LV00002B/170/P

9 780692 721033